PRAISE FOR
DREAM WEAVER

"Jenny Jing Zhu is one of the most inspiring and driven people I've met, and that's echoed in every page of *Dream Weaver*. Her journey from a small village in China to leading a successful company in the U.S. is filled with lessons on perseverance, making bold choices, and following your vision no matter the odds. It's a blueprint for anyone with big dreams and the determination to make them happen."

-**DREW SCOTT**, Founder Scott Brothers Global/Property Brothers

"I once asked the legendary Quincy Jones why some talented musicians succeed while others don't. His answer was a single word: personality. Indeed, success and failure in life often come down to personality—and that's certainly true of Jenny Jing Zhu. She has the most delightful personality I know, like a ray of sunshine—always happy and optimistic about people and events. People love being around her and working with her.

Despite facing many life challenges, she maintains a remarkable attitude. Her "go-forward" spirit propels her to succeed, and her curiosity drives her to explore opportunities others might overlook. Jenny is a truly special and inspiring woman. Her book is a must-read for any young, aspiring entrepreneur!"

—**YUE-SAI KAN**, Fashion Icon, Successful Entrepreneur, Best-Selling
Author, and World-Renowned Philanthropist

"The first time I met Jenny and learned about her journey—rising from poverty in China to build a successful business in America—I was truly inspired. She strikes the perfect balance between being laid-back and a fierce go-getter, showing kindness and dedication in everything she does. Jenny is a true role model, and I'm so proud to call her my friend. If you want to feel inspired and empowered, read her book."

- **KIM CLIJSTERS**, Former World No. 1 Tennis Player, Four-Time Grand
Slam Champion, and International Tennis Hall of Fame Inductee

"Jenny's life journey has been nothing short of extraordinary. From humble beginnings to building an incredible life in the U.S., her story is one of resilience, vision, and unstoppable courage. As a leader, she combines fierce determination with genuine heart and passion—a rare quality that makes her both inspiring and unforgettable. *Dream Weaver* is a testament to the remarkable strength it takes to pursue one's aspirations against all odds, and a powerful reminder for anyone who has faith in oneself and dares to dream big."

– CAMILLE BURNS, CEO Women Presidents Organization

"I have known Jenny Zhu all my life (spoiler alert, I'm her son), and if I could describe her in one word, it would be stubborn or, more endearingly, tenacious, but just one word isn't near enough. When she put her mind to coming to America without a lick of English, she was bold. When she decided to stay in America as a single mother with her slightly upgraded 'Jinglish,' she was brave. To then start a company amid the 2008 financial crisis, she was insane. And as a mother, she's the best.

Growing up, I never really experienced a 'normal' family. My mom was divorced twice, and my biological father lives in China. But that never seemed like an issue for me. I still had loving parents, Mom, Dad, and Ba Ba (that's dad in Chinese), and I never felt like I missed out on anything. I still had parents who loved me, even if it wasn't under traditional circumstances, in fact, I had one extra parent that loved and supported me, along with an entire tree of relatives that I love and hold as my own. I couldn't imagine anything different or be more grateful for all that I call family—and getting to celebrate three Christmases is a win-win in my book!

Against overwhelming odds, my mom prevailed, and amid her mountain of disadvantages, she found her strength. This is a book about overcoming, and I have learned so much about my mom that I never would have known. She's my biggest inspiration, and I hope you enjoy."

– DAREN CHEN, Jenny's Son

DREAM WEAVER

INDIGORIVER
PUBLISHING

DREAM WEAVER

HOW TO FIND STRENGTH & PURPOSE IN LIFE'S TWISTS AND TURNS

JENNY JING ZHU

FOUNDER OF LUSH DECOR

Dream Weaver: How to Find Strength and Purpose in Life's Twists and Turns

© 2025 by Jenny Jing Zhu

Library of Congress Control Number: 2024914564

ISBN: 978-1-964686-03-5 (paperback)   978-1-964686-02-8 (hardcover)
        978-1-964686-04-2 (ebook)

This is a work of creative non-fiction. All the events in this memoir are true to the best of the author's memory. Some names, geographic locations, physical character-istics, and other identifying features have been changed where applicable to protect the privacy of certain individuals. The author in no way represents any company, corporation, or brand mentioned herein except her own. The views expressed in this memoir are solely those of the author.

Editors: Deborah Froese, Stephanie Thompson
Cover and Interior Design: Emma Elzinga

Printed in the United States of America

First Edition

3 West Garden Street, Ste. 718
Pensacola, FL 32502
www.indigoriverpublishing.com

Ordering Information:

Quantity sales: Special discounts are available on quantity purchases by corporations, associations, and others. For details, contact the publisher at the address above.

Orders by US trade bookstores and wholesalers: Please contact the publisher at the address above.

With Indigo River Publishing, you can always expect great books, strong voices, and meaningful messages. Most importantly, you'll always find . . . *words worth reading.*

"Dreaming isn't just about reaching the stars. It's about believing in yourself, taking the first step, then one foot after another, and having faith that the path will unfold."

-JENNY JING ZHU

To my two children: my son, Daren, who inspires me to grow as a mother, and my daughter, Lush Decor, for providing the spark for my dreams and the foundation on which to build them.

And to my family, my Lush Decor team, and the incredible women and immigrants who inspire me daily—thank you for your love, strength, and belief in the power of dreams.

May we all keep weaving dreams, creating stories that empower, connect, and uplift us all.

INTRODUCTION

THE FIRST TIME I stepped onto American soil, night blanketed the sky. I couldn't see anything. Blindness forced all my other senses into overdrive, and the foreign, pungent odor of pine trees overwhelmed me. San Francisco smelled nothing like the streets of Beijing where the aroma of roasted chestnuts and the rich, savory scent of Peking duck from street vendors filled the air. With my first breath of San Francisco air, the woody, spiced-pine perfume found a permanent place in my memory. The unmistakable scent and the anxiety pounding in my chest escorted me as I plunged headlong into the unknown.

Without friends or a community, I had nothing to do but sit in the small apartment my husband shared with his American law school classmate and watch television programs I did not understand. My companion visa and my inability to communicate prevented me from getting a job. Within days, I realized I had to find something to occupy my brain before I went crazy.

Once again, I found myself starting a new journey while facing a significant obstacle. At the time, though, I didn't see it that way. In fact, it wasn't until I began writing this book that I realized how many obstacles I have overcome during the course of my life. The funny thing is, I was the only one who did not see them as obstacles. My friends called me delusional because I always envisioned the beautiful scene beyond the brick wall standing in my way, at the top of the mountain I had to climb.

Perhaps naivete or stubborn determination blinded me to the realities of my situation. But I discovered the power of looking at obstacles from a different angle. An obstacle could provide an opportunity to take a new path, overcome limitations, and grow stronger. Obstacles can reveal the very thread necessary for success. For me, learning to recognize such threads when they appeared took time and patience. So did the skill of weaving them into a tapestry that would support me as my dreams became reality.

Dream Weaver shares the the precious threads of experience I discovered through the hardships I faced in business and in life. I hope you find inspiration in the childhood moment that ignited my passion for independence and following my dreams and in the countless heart-wrenching lessons that strengthened my intuition.

As a little girl, I found inspiration in the stories of women who went before me. My grandma was the first woman to inspire me. In my village, we grew cotton, hand-picked it, and spun it into thread. Then women like my grandma wove it into fabric. Sitting at Grandma's feet, I would watch in awe as her hands danced across colorful threads weaving traditional fabric, stories, and dreams together on an old wooden loom under an oil lamp.

By sharing my journey from my birth in a village lacking basic services such as electricity and indoor plumbing to navigating challenges as a first-generation immigrant and female entrepreneur, I hope to ignite a spark within you too.

It wasn't until later in my life that the significance of my grandma's loom became clear to me. The idea of weaving my life together like a resilient, visionary, and beautiful tapestry became a powerful visual. I picked up many threads throughout my life; independence, intuition, gratitude, love, trust, passion, determination, self-confidence—and more. As I wove them together, the tapestry of my life grew stronger. It caught me when I stumbled and fell. When I plummeted toward rock bottom, it became the safety net that saved me from crashing. It provided a soft place to land and regroup.

I stand as a testament to the power of perseverance and vision, and the courage to transform dreams, weaving them into reality. I want to show you that no matter the outcome, you should always try, and always do your best. For those who grapple with challenges, doubt, and fear, those who see giving up as their only option, I hope my journey can shine some light on your path. May it encourage you to weave your threads of experience into a unique, resilient, and beautiful life tapestry too.

CHAPTER 1

THE LONG FLIGHT from the place I had never left before exhausted me. The farther away I moved from home, the farther away I moved from my identity.

That part came as a surprise. Before I left Beijing, my logical mind mulled over details about how life would be different in San Francisco. I thought mostly of language and culture. I didn't anticipate how different everything else would be too: the powerful scent of pine trees, the city sounds, the crazy hilly streets, the wildly high prices, and the free-spirited way people lived and smoked marijuana. In my first few hours on American soil, these differences overwhelmed me. A sense of uncertainty mixed with fear of the unknown and drove home the feeling that I was an alien—not just from another country but from another planet.

Searching the crowded airline terminal through the melting pot of diverse faces, I held my breath until I spotted Wei, my husband of six months, waiting at the bottom of a long escalator. We'd only known each other for five days before he proposed marriage. A small informal wedding, a few short weeks together, and I had taken him to the airport for a flight to San Francisco where he would attend law school. I planned to take a few months to settle my business and personal affairs in Beijing before joining him in America.

"It will be like an adventure," he had said.

In two years, we would return to Beijing. He would get a job at a law firm or maybe start his own. But two years seemed like a lifetime in that moment, gazing down the escalator at a virtual stranger.

At the age of twenty-six, I had never traveled outside of China, had never been married before, and spoke only two English phrases: "hello" and "nice to meet you." When I headed for San Francisco, I left a string of small but successful business ventures behind. I left my vibrant social life behind. I left my parents and brother behind too. Without realizing it, I also left my independence behind. Overnight I became two years old again. I had to communicate with my hands, pointing and gesturing as I struggled to get my message across.

My new husband smiled broadly as I stepped off the escalator and met me with a hug. I hoped his presence would relieve some of my anxiety, but it had little effect. His roommate, Patrick, shook my hand and gave me a polite hug. They led me to the baggage carousel, talking and laughing in English as I silently followed behind.

Is this how it's going to be? Left out of every conversation?

My new reality quickly set in.

From the back seat of Patrick's car, I stared out the window at the midnight sky. Even the flicker of moonlight on waves in the San Francisco Bay seemed different from anything I'd seen before. When Patrick pulled the car into a spot along the street in front of a three-story row house, newness tumbled into anxiety, and my heart sank. I had hoped that making it safely from China to the apartment we were sharing with Patrick and his wife would give me a sense of relief. No such luck.

My breathing grew shallow as we climbed the narrow staircase to the second floor. Patrick's wife, Sebrina, was also an immigrant. She came from France. She greeted me with a sincere hug and led me to our room. I honestly didn't even look around the apartment.

My husband and I said our good nights. It was already after one a.m. local time, but just four p.m. in my Chinese body. When my husband turned out the bedside light, my eyes remained wide open as my heart raced. It would be a long night.

✳

A salty, meaty smell worked its way under the door of the small bed we shared in the room of that second-floor apartment.

"What is that?" I sat up abruptly to find myself alone. I shuffled to the kitchen, trying to shake off the jet lag that fogged my brain. Wei had already dressed for class and stood there with Patrick and Sebrina.

"What are you cooking?" I asked in Mandarin, the only language I knew.

Wei greeted me with a smile. "Bacon and eggs."

In my village, we would slaughter a pig or goat once a year to celebrate Chinese New Year, but never on a random weekday, and never for breakfast. It was so foreign to think of eating meat with no sign of the noodles, dumplings, or steamed buns my stomach was accustomed to.

Welcome to Day One, I thought.

In the few minutes before Wei rushed out with our new roommates to start his day, he explained a few things to me. "Press this button to turn on the TV. Here's a key; be sure to lock the door if you go out. The market is a few blocks down the street. We'll be back around four."

The door closed behind them, leaving me alone.

"Go out? Are you crazy?" I thought out loud. I flopped my exhausted body onto the couch and surveyed the surroundings. The walls and decor were mostly bare but not unkempt. The TV was not that big, but it was bulky. In those days, TVs were deeper than they were wide.

A cluster of Patrick and Sebrina's framed wedding pictures hung neatly on the wall above the TV, along with vacation scenes and candid group photos of what I assumed were extended family. I pulled a hand-knitted blanket off the back of the couch and wrapped it around my shoulders. I'd never seen a blanket like that, knitted and so thick, but it offered comfort—exactly what I needed at that moment.

Exhaustion, overwhelm, and anxiety began to cut their way through my brain fog. Never in my twenty-six years had I felt so helpless and vulnerable. The independent, rebellious, risk-taking me I had fought so hard for seemed to slip through my hands as effortlessly as the water that flowed from the kitchen faucet.

✳

Summertime in Caolou, the remote village in the Shandong Province of China where I spent my childhood, brought with it a semi-tropical monsoon climate that made working conditions in the fields grueling, especially for a young child. My family did some crop tending in the late afternoons, but the humidity, our school, and my parents' full-time jobs meant we mostly worked in the moonlight. The vivid glow of a full moon made midnight weeding, watering, or harvesting the cotton crop a bit easier. The melodic rustle of bushes being picked clean of the snowy white cotton bolls blended easily with my mother's rhythmic breathing. It created the sound that will forever define harvest for me.

My earliest memory took root at age five when I disappeared under a giant straw gathering basket that my mother strapped over my small shoulders.

"Jing-Jing, I can hardly see you! It looks like the gathering basket is moving by itself," Mother teased. It would not be the only time in my life that I would disappear under an engulfing shadow.

A bout of misdiagnosed meningitis that nearly ended my life at age three gave my body the early challenge of a slow start. I had become very sick with a high fever, waking only to vomit.

Meningitis was common at the time. So were lineups to see a doctor.

"It's just a virus. You can take her home." Overwhelmed, the doctor at the local clinic moved from patient to patient as quickly as possible.

"Is everything okay with Jing?" A family friend, a doctor who happened to be at the clinic, stopped us on our way out. Mother, holding my limp body in her arms, provided a brief explanation of my condition. While they talked, I started having a seizure-like episode.

"Let me have a quick look at her." Our family friend glanced at the rash on my chest and noted my overall lethargy. "She is not well. Stay right here." He ran out of the room to get a dose of medicine and arranged for me to be moved by ambulance to the city hospital.

After examining me, the city doctor delivered a grim diagnosis. "If she cannot wake up, there is nothing we can do."

Of the seven children in that hospital ward who were battling the same condition, I am the only one who survived. A miracle. I may have had some hardships as a small child, but being undersized was a gift in comparison to the other children's fate. I think it's where my fighter instinct was born. Somehow, I knew early in life that I had to prove myself.

All the village kids would play so hard together, running and chasing each other. We made toys out of sticks and bags. When suppertime arrived, our parents yelled for us to come home. Our lives may have been simple, but we never felt we were missing anything. People were happy with very little.

When harvesting finished, people took naps in the sun because they had nothing else to do. That's how they relaxed after all the hard work was done. Outside of the harvest season, people gathered in the center of the village to have lunch and gossip and laugh. Most of the villagers had simple ambitions: working the fields by day, a full belly at night.

Winter months were always harsh and unforgiving, especially in our small village where resources like food were scarce. We often had to rely on our wit and imagination to survive. I vividly remember the luxury of acquiring a basket of yellow apples during the winter months. What an irresistible aroma those yellow apples had, a distinct fragrance that filled the room, so pleasant that it made me salivate. The flesh of the yellow apple was crisp, sweet, and juicy, every bite a burst of flavor in my mouth. Yellow apples were rare. We could only enjoy them during special occasions like the Chinese New Year, the Lunar Festival, or when we had guests over. No wonder we savored every single bite!

Mother would place the yellow apples in a small basket and carefully wrap them in red paper to present them as gifts. The presentation of these yellow apples was as important as their taste. Those gifts of yellow apples contributed to our family's status. Our tiny village consisted of about three hundred people living in simple houses with dirt floors, no electricity, and a hole in our yards that served as our toilets. Even though we lived like they did, people in the village considered us a rich and highly respected family. My mother was a schoolteacher, and my father worked for the government. Their jobs put us in the working class with stable salaries.

Father spent a lot of time away, so child-rearing and crop tending fell almost entirely on my mother's shoulders. Her parents had arranged and sanctioned their marriage. They believed my mother would benefit from belonging to the working class through my father's societal stature.

In those days, China frowned upon entrepreneurship. My maternal grandfather ran a small manufacturing business making and bottling vinegar. My father served the country by working for the government. Marrying him meant Mother would share in his favorable status. Her parents allowed her to complete high school, but their decision for her to marry dashed any dreams of bigger things. She kept her resentment neatly tucked away, but it never left.

I have no doubt her resentment sometimes enhanced the fury of the frequent spankings delivered to my backside. Mother joked that hitting my butt wouldn't cause injuries. She didn't handle her anger well, but she did her best. She drew upon her capacity for hard work and always strove to improve.

Our Chinese family tucked love away. We lived a good life, but showing affection wasn't part of the culture. As an adult, I always wanted to break that barrier between my parents and I, to hug and love them more. But I still find it stressful to talk with Mother and often find an excuse to hang up the phone to avoid any awkward attempts at "I love you."

*

Do you remember your first serious dream? A bike merchant unknowingly inspired mine at the tender age of six. He drove the Chinese equivalent of an ice cream truck, riding his bicycle along the fields at dusk and ringing the bell attached to the handlebars. A long tail-like plume of dust rose up behind him, taking on an eerie glow in the fading sunlight. A large box strapped to the back of the bike held sweet icy treats we called ice cubes. Mostly made of ice with some sugar and flavoring, we thought they were a taste of heaven. They worked magic on our parched, dirt-rimmed mouths. That bell made all the kids in the village drop their baskets and run to meet him. Mother rarely gave me money to get one, even though we were "rich."

"Frivolous spending is bad," she would lecture my little brother and me.

Frustrated by my situation, my little brain started churning. If only I had my own money, I could get all the ice cubes I want! And right there, on a blistering summer evening in a cotton field on the outskirts of a remote village in Shangdong Province, an entrepreneur was born. I didn't know that word yet, or that my fierce independence had been set ablaze with no chance of turning back.

It's funny to me to think about how my independence blossomed so early. I often wonder about the exasperation my poor mother must have endured raising "Little Jing," as I was known, the only wild child in the village. These days, I would be labeled as a spirited child. Mother was never that politically correct.

On my daily walk to school, I would pass by a small masonry factory near the village center, a large one-story building that housed a kiln to bake bricks. A row of large doorways lined one side. Finished bricks were stacked in those doorways, waiting to be loaded onto a flatbed truck for delivery to a building site. Villagers lined up to load the bricks, a welcomed source of income for many. Carrying the bricks by hand to the flatbed truck earned them a fen, similar to a penny, for each brick they loaded.

I'd never paid much attention to that line and the masonry truck—until the yearning for unlimited ice cubes struck. My six-year-old brain shifted perspective.

If they can get paid for loading bricks, why not me? I can carry bricks!

I always tried to overcome my size issue of being deemed too small.

I wanted to do my part and prove I could do it well. It was the first time the thread of independence appeared, making a very public appearance as I got in line with the adults. I was unaware of its significance at the time and had no idea about what to do with a thread that would add so much texture to my life's tapestry.

I was small, but quick, making twice as many trips as the adults could, which annoyed some of them. I, however, felt overjoyed as the fen piled up in my pocket. And I was hooked. Okay, maybe a little obsessed. What kid wouldn't be? The independence and the freedom it gave me were intoxicating. I didn't have to ask permission. I was the boss of me, and it felt good all the way to my toes. While my village playmates chased each other around, I made money and ate my fill of ice cubes.

At first, Mother didn't know about my newfound money-making endeavor. But one of the village women saw Mother at the market one morning and made a point of telling her about my antics. Then the spankings began. At least, that is my earliest recollection of getting spanked. I have no doubt Mother couldn't hide her shock. And finding out that I was the big story in the village gossip circles only added to her fury.

"That work is for adults! You stay away!" Her sharp tone matched the sting lingering on my backside. The sense of embarrassment she felt knowing her child took income from adults was lost on me.

What's the big deal? I wondered.

As my independence blossomed, Mother knew only one response in her effort to control me. In our house, her form of discipline was just that: discipline. I think she wanted to beat the stubbornness out of me, but physical discipline only deepened my resolve. More importantly, the thread of entrepreneurship that had poked out a bit too early was tucked away.

Mother and I butted heads often because I always argued my point. The intensity of the beatings increased with my age and obstinate attitude. Mother's bitterness about her prearranged marriage also contributed. She remained stuck in the village while her brothers and sisters went to the city, pursuing the lives they desired. Mother felt trapped, and her anger simmered just below the surface. Unfortunately, therapy was unheard of back then, but she did her best with the knowledge she had to help me grow up as "normal" as possible.

Father supported her childrearing choices but work often kept him away, leaving my management to her. "I'm going to live long enough to see you regret this!" he often remarked about my stubbornness and choices.

We didn't have conversations during my childhood; he just gave me his opinion. That resulted in a weak relationship between us.

My brother, younger by three years, was the smart one. The good child. He had a totally different personality from me. Shy, he often hid when visitors came to our house. He proved much better at listening and following the rules, and I don't think he ever received a spanking. He would apologize immediately if he got into trouble, but not me. I was the black sheep in the family.

My relationship with my grandma provided a safe space to be myself; she withheld her opinions about my rebellious spirit. I was in awe of her. On our humble dirt floor, my grandma took center stage with her wooden loom. Employing the ancient Chinese method, one that has remained unchanged through centuries, her seasoned hands transformed raw cotton into fabric. With every twist and turn, her fingers danced, weaving stories, not just cloth. She told tales of our ancestors, how their attire was made with immense love and patience, and how each thread echoed the spirit of the land and the diligence of its people.

As a little girl, I found those weaving sessions mesmerizing. It wasn't just about the art of creating fabric but delving deep into its very essence. To me, it was pure art, rooted in tradition, emotion, and memory. I used to sneak onto the loom and try to use it, messing up my grandma's work in the process. The sound of the weave on the wood and the image of her petite feet pushing the pedals was forever imprinted in my mind. That loom was more than just a tool; it was the key that would eventually unlock my dreams for the future.

✳

My rebellious and independent spirit blossomed during my childhood. It didn't take long for it to feel threatened during my first week in San Francisco. Our first significant marital spat was heating up, and I could feel an explosion coming on.

Before my arrival, Wei and Patrick had responded on my behalf to a newspaper ad by a young couple seeking a nanny for their soon-to-be-born baby.

"I don't know how to take care of a baby!" I protested.

But my companion visa prohibited me from getting paid, and we didn't have much money, so Wei and Patrick had arranged for us to live in the couple's in-law apartment in exchange for my childcare services. I thought the arrangement was fair, but my lack of English kept me out of the decision-making, which didn't sit well with my fierce independence. It made me feel 100 percent dependent on Wei, like a kid who needed her parents' help to get that first job.

Wei didn't force me to take the nanny job. I knew it made good sense, and it offered a good opportunity to learn about the culture, but caring for the baby really worried me.

Back in Beijing, I had more money than Wei. I remember telling him, "It's okay. If this doesn't work, you still have me." I always felt my money would allow us to live comfortably. The lack of income put me in a position of weakness. I didn't like it.

Disagreements and tension were rare in our young marriage, but Patrick and Sebrina knew something was up one night when I failed to muffle my frustration in our tiny corner bedroom. It's easy to identify anger in any language. Wei wanted me to learn American culture. He thought being a nanny was a good way for me to interact with real America and learn English. Although the idea made sense, the responsibility that came with it filled me with anxiety. I had no ability to express my sense of weakness to him. I felt hopeless and helpless at the same time, and that made me angry It created an awkward moment for us.

To make matters worse, homesickness fueled my anxiety. The arrival of the year 2000 ushered in the twenty-first century. Watching the world celebrate on TV, I felt so alone without my friends and the vibrant social life I had enjoyed back in Beijing. I imagined them all out partying.

"I need to be alone. I'm going out for a walk," I snapped, grabbing the key and striding toward the door—even though it was after ten p.m.

With my tomboy ways still intact, I jumped down three or four stairs at a time until I reached the ground floor and burst through the front entry of our apartment building. The night air felt noticeably cooler than daytime. Wind scooped salty ocean air off the San Francisco Bay and spread it up the hillside into our predominantly white neighborhood. I bolted at first, sprinting up the steep incline of the empty sidewalk, seeking some release from the anxiety and frustration consuming me.

I loved playing sports in high school. A growth spurt in my early teens eliminated the disadvantage of my previously undersized body. Athletic abilities blossomed in my slender new five-foot, eight-inch frame. Competition and the thrill of a win were like rocket fuel for me. But as I ran up that steep San Francisco sidewalk, my stomach did a flip the same way it had back at school when I threw up after a 5000-meter race. I hated running back then, but I wanted to win, to beat my competitors to the finish line. This time, I wanted to win by outrunning my frustration. I didn't care who saw me or what I looked like; I just needed to escape. That harvest-gathering basket from my childhood paled in comparison to the shadow engulfing me now.

Reaching the crest of the hill, I bent over breathing hard, fighting the urge to puke, and realizing just how out of shape I had become. I didn't know where I was going; I just walked into the night. Very dangerous for a noticeably tall Asian woman who could only speak a few basic words in English, but there I was.

Only a few days earlier, Wei and I became separated on the jam-packed subway train, and I got off at the wrong stop. He had to come back to get me. Bursting with fear and anxiety, I stood like a stone on the platform, waiting to be rescued.

But that night, I walked on.

The affluent Buena Vista neighborhood was quiet at that hour with only the occasional car making its way to a place called home. As I walked, the fury began clearing from my eyes and mind. I looked through glowing windows as I passed. Lamps on side tables filled the window frames with light, filtered by sheer draperies and casting a warmth I could almost feel. It was home for someone; it just wasn't home for me. I felt empty and alone. If I disappeared, no one would even notice.

Never in my young life had I felt so isolated. I didn't know who I was anymore. The only person I had to rely on was Wei. He didn't understand my growing anxiety over the loss of my identity and independence. He spoke English better than I did; he'd been here for six months, and he came to the US with a clear purpose. His immigrant experience unfolded in a very different way from mine.

As my emotions settled, I began to contemplate my situation. At that moment, in this foreign country, I had nothing. I had boldly embraced our international move the same way I had previously embraced my move from Caolou to Beijing for a job. I always loved the feeling of risk-taking. I didn't thoroughly think through a risk, I just took it. I loved the goosebumps that rose from a new idea, the thrill, and the adventure. Though the reality checks were often hard, I just kept on going. But in San Francisco, I had no financial independence or a place of my own to live.

I wished one of those warm, glowing windows were mine.

That moment became etched in my memory as one of the most frightening experiences in my life here in the US.

Independence is a word with such a big meaning. There are so many choices to make in the tradeoff for self sufficiency, so much to lose. It was the first time my thread of independence felt truly strained. *Would it break?* At that moment, I knew I had to get my life back. I had forged my independence before; now it was time to dig deep again.

CHAPTER 2

LOOKING BACK, I realize exploring my independence came naturally. Yes, Mother spanked me and argued vehemently when I pushed her boundaries, but that was really the worst of it.

After elementary school, my parents sent me to a boarding school in a small nearby town, probably in part to quell the arguments. But it was also likely Mother's attempt to give me more than a customary education. I defied more cultural expectations by attending high school. Girls in villages like mine rarely stayed in the education system beyond middle school. They tended to marry young and spent their lives helping care for the crops and run the household. Mother wanted more for me. I believe it was her way of living out her dreams for both herself and me.

Where I grew up, boys were more important than girls. At the time, I didn't realize just how much this pervasive cultural norm shaped my tomboy mindset, stubborn determination, and rebellious spirit. I always felt like I was capable of doing everything a boy could do: make a few pennies, cut grass, help my parents. I was hellbent on defying that norm, to prove myself. I am not less than anyone. I can be anything I want. If other people can do it, I have no reason not to do it too, and I have every reason to do even better.

Boarding school was a dream come true. I lived in a big dorm room with ten girls and bunk beds. It felt like a giant sleepover. The dorms had no heat, no air conditioning, and no indoor plumbing. I had to wash my own clothes. That task seemed a small price to pay for the sheer joy the independence boarding school gave me. My already outgoing personality blossomed.

Mother's spankings stopped once I went to boarding school. I guess the distance helped because my parents missed me. Each time I returned home after a month away, Mother prepared the food I loved and spoiled me until I headed back to school again.

My aunt lived near the school, so I visited her once a week. Her garden produced enough vegetables to sell at the local marketplace. I loved going with her to the market, where she would let me collect and count the money. After several years lying dormant, my entrepreneurial thread was being teased out again.

"Jing-Jing, you are very good with the customers," she would tell me, giving me a gentle pat on the shoulder. "And very good at counting the money!"

It made both of us laugh.

Once the school realized I had athletic ability, they put me on every team they had: track and field, volleyball, and badminton. Being small didn't matter anymore because my determination was bigger than my competitors'. I still hold a school record in the high jump and a volleyball championship.

After freshman year, students chose one of two concentrations of study, either liberal arts, which focused on history, political science, and geography; or natural science, which focused on physics, chemistry, and biology.

"You are to study natural sciences, Jing-Jing," Mother directed during one of my monthly visits. She made it clear the decision was final. I had no choice. She believed I would have more opportunities to find a job as a schoolteacher if I majored in math and sciences. I soon discovered something else I would need to overcome. Natural sciences did not jive with the way my brain worked. I just didn't get it. Despite this obstacle, I made it into the top twenty in my class.

The difficulty I had in school helped define my motto to always do my best, no matter what.

Mother was so proud and excited for me to go to college. She wanted me to become a teacher, following in her footsteps. I didn't share her enthusiasm. I just couldn't deal with the status quo or the idea of being confined to a classroom.. Teaching didn't seem adventurous enough for my spirit. I didn't feel I had explored enough to give anything back. Evolving and learning were my passions.

I kept all those thoughts to myself for a while.

The National College Entrance Exam lasts about nine hours over two or three days. They are held once per year in mainland China, and your score determines the handful of colleges you can attend. I didn't perform well. Based on my score, I had few options, and that meant choosing between a couple of mediocre colleges to become a teacher. College began to feel more like a prison sentence than an opportunity.

Once again, my brain and independence kicked in. Earlier in the school year, a family member of a classmate had been murdered, leaving us all a bit shaken. I wanted to do something. I wanted to help them. Anger and compassion flared, so I decided to become a detective. I forged ahead with my plan, never mentioning it to my parents. First, I had to apply to attend the detectives' academy. Next, I had to keep looking for alternative careers because I didn't get accepted.

But I didn't have to look too far for my next inspiration. Have you ever experienced a moment when something simple changed the direction of your life? For me, it came in the form of a magazine article about a young woman who went to Shenzhen to become an entrepreneur. She came from a very humble background and a small village just like mine. The story clicked something in my brain, opening the floodgates of my dreams. The picture of her standing in front of her business with an education similar to mine, discovering how much she had achieved, and the fearless look in her eyes—it all captivated me. I saw myself in her story, and I knew I could make my own money like I had as a child. It was the first time I thought about entrepreneurship as the path to the independence I so desperately wanted. I could hardly contain my excitement. It provided the spark I needed. I realized I needed to get out of the village, explore the big city, and find a job to become a businesswoman just like her. The thread of entrepreneurship brought with it the thread of risk-taking and I fell in love with both of them.

Announcing that I was not going to college made Mother's blood boil. "That is not acceptable!" she shouted.

After a long, fiery exchange, Mother came up with a compromise. "If you don't like the college we chose, you can take the test again next year to get into a better school."

"I don't want to waste my time. I want to get out of this village," I replied.

At eighteen, I was ready to get a job and expand my horizons. A trip to Beijing in fourth grade had opened my eyes to another larger world, and I wanted more of it. I remember seeing a toilet for the first time during that trip. It took me a few days to figure out how to use the damn thing, but I found it pretty amazing.

"I want to get a job in Beijing," I said.

That statement set Mother off again. She wouldn't even consider it. Our fighting intensified, and we stopped talking to each other for a few months. To further my point and anger her even more, I refused to eat the meals she made for me. It touched a nerve in her. I became really good at doing that.

By this time, Mother had informed my father of my desire, and he sided with her, joining the battle.

"You are ruining your life!" he said, adding to their argument. "You will fail miserably and come back home empty-handed."

The only option they understood for my life was the traditional route of attending college to become a teacher with a stable salary. I had no interest, and they had no hope. I just wanted to make a lot of money to prove my way could be stable too.

I'm so frustrated. Where can I go to escape?

Xiujun and I had been friends since high school, and we shared similar frustrations, so I ran away to her house which was a few miles away in a neighboring village. It didn't take Mother long to figure out where I went. She and my father came to get me. As parents, they were embarrassed to have their daughter misbehave and run away. But that was my goal. I wanted them to feel embarrassed when they knocked on Xiujun's door. I wanted them to feel so badly about my behavior that they would let me go to Beijing.

At first, they held fast. Determined not to give in, I ran away a few more times, hiding in fields of crops, watching them walk by as they called my name. Eventually I would relent and return home.

One day, Mother called me to the kitchen where my father sat stone-faced, angry and crushed by my behavior. They had based their dreams on my future, and I disappointed them.

"You will fail, Jing-Jing."

Father's negative words stung, but I bit my tongue.

Mother cleared her throat to redirect the conversation. "We've decided to let you go with my brother in Beijing. He made arrangements for you to work at the front desk of a government hotel."

Years later, I came to understand my behavior had crushed their dreams and their pride. The entire village thought I was very bright and expected me to be the first girl from the village to go to college. That would have been a significant point of pride for my parents. My resistance delivered them a tremendous blow. Other people viewed my choice negatively too. I wanted to prove them all wrong. I wanted to show them just how strong my newfound thread of risk-taking really was.

I promised Mother that I would start college at night while working days at the hotel to earn money. I intended to make lots of money, a quest driven by my lifelong desire to improve my family's fate. No one gave me that responsibility; I just took it upon myself early in life. I'm not sure why I gave myself that kind of pressure, but it came naturally. It drove me. It was just something I needed to do. That drive helped me discover the thread of family which I knew had to be woven into whatever I did in my life.

Moving to a city, taking a menial job, opting for night school, and forging my own path without the full support of my family meant taking a big risk. Some said the risk was too big. I didn't see it that way. I saw it as an exciting next step in my journey.

❋

"Are you ready to go?" Wei paused at the front door of the apartment, his hand grasping the handle. He didn't like being late for class.

After the tense moment we had shared in our bedroom and my late-night walk through the neighborhood, Wei wanted to support me. He suggested I go to campus with him and spend time at the library instead of staying at the apartment by myself with little to do. Alone at the apartment, I escaped by walking down the big hill and then climbing all the way back up with enormous bags of groceries filled with comfort food. In this different world where I felt as though I didn't belong, eating was a welcome distraction.

I rushed to clear the breakfast dishes and grabbed my coat, excited to visit Wei's law school and an actual college campus. A large modern granite and glass building, the library Wei told me about sat on the edge of a plaza. I remember how beautiful the plaza was, lined by a mixture of modern and classical structures, pale yellow and glass dominating the architecture. Pavers covered most of the space outside the library, and students occupied a cluster of iron patio tables and chairs, enjoying their coffee in the morning sun.

The main library doors opened into a dramatic vaulted glass atrium with tile flooring. Deep red leather chairs set in conversation groups around oversized block design coffee tables drew me in with a modern but warm and welcoming vibe. Wei signed me in as a guest and showed me where the restrooms were.

"See you at four," he said over his shoulder as he hurried off to class.

I stayed in that library all day because I still couldn't speak English and was too afraid to go anywhere else. I didn't have the courage to brave unfamiliar surroundings, so I spent my time browsing through books and trying to absorb as much English as possible. The strong, earthy smell of aged bound paper I encountered there would stay with me throughout my life, just like the scent of pine.

Uneasiness, anxiety, and excitement tumbled around inside me like socks in a dryer. I was accustomed to overcoming hard things with sheer determination. The language barrier would prove to be a formidable opponent. The English classes I took in Beijing were such a waste; I retained very little and had no place to practice speaking English in Beijing.

People spoke so much faster in America! When Patrick suggested I attend a local college that offered free English lessons, I jumped at the opportunity. Once lessons began, I borrowed books from the library and watched lots of PBS shows to speed up my learning. It was still a tedious process, but I forced myself to learn.

Learning English would be my ticket back to the independence I cherished in China.

Do your best, no matter what.

❋

Beijing taught me a lot. At age nineteen, moving from the village to the city was the biggest step I had ever taken in my young life. The move from the village to the boarding school had felt big, but moving to the city brought me into adulthood. At nineteen, I embraced it boldly, happy to be free of Mother's arguments and control.

My uncle arranged for me to live in one of the hotel rooms with three other girls as part of my pay. A nasty storm welcomed me to my very first night of life in a big city. Wind gusts and heavy rain beat the window and made the building groan. I'd never heard anything like it before. Sitting in that small hotel room, I clutched my pillow tight to stop shaking while my new roommates slept through it all. It was frightening.

This sucks.

The next morning, I awoke early and realized I was fine. I told myself things would get better as I adjusted to my new surroundings.

✻

"You will attend the front desk when the clerk takes lunch or a break. The rest of the time, you will clean rooms."

Xie, the thirty-something woman who was our supervisor, was direct with my new roommates and me.

What? This isn't what I thought my job would be. I hate cleaning! I bit my tongue. *It doesn't matter. This is what I fought for; it's the life I want. It will all work out.*

Xie showed us to the large closet housing the cleaning supplies and introduced us to Min, a delightful woman in her late twenties with a gentle smile. Min had been head housekeeper for several years.

"Min will teach you how to do the cleaning," Xie said. "Pay attention. I want it done thoroughly."

Min showed us how to clean toilets, mop floors, strip the beds, and where to deposit soiled linens.

"You are getting really good at toilet cleaning," she would tell me with a wink.

Her patience and good-spirited ribbing helped with the drudgery of the work. Over time, Xie softened her tone, taking extra time to teach me the finer points of working the front desk. She recognized my people skills. I think she was grooming me to move up to a role with more responsibility, but I had already conjured up a bigger vision than working at the front desk.

By the end of the first week, my hatred for every part of the housekeeping work had blossomed. The reaction from a group of guests who walked by one morning really set me off. As I finished mopping up one half of the hallway floor, they intentionally walked over it. One man dropped a gum wrapper.

"You missed a spot," he said.

The entire group broke out in laughter. They showed no respect for me or the work I had done, instead choosing to look down on those who did manual labor. I felt their judgment, and I seethed with anger. It was a learning moment. To this day, I have great appreciation for those who do this work and how hard they work to make our lives nicer. That experience helped me weave the threads of awareness and gratitude into my life. I take nothing and no one for granted.

As I mopped, I thought about the magazine article featuring the entrepreneur from a small village like mine, the woman who started a business. It fueled an obsession to figure out what kind of business I could start. In the evenings, Xie allowed me to read discarded newspapers in the hotel lobby, so I took the opportunity to look for affordable certifications I could complete quickly. As my savings steadily grew, it made sense to me to use them wisely.

"Oh, this looks interesting." I thought out loud, alone in the lobby one evening. "Become licensed to provide cosmetic skin care treatments and services such as facials, hair removal, and makeup application. Why not? I can do that."

I used the same reasoning I drew upon to carry bricks as a six-year-old. I chuckled at the thought. I had always been a tomboy, but since coming to Beijing, I realized how good it felt to dress up and put on lipstick. It was the first time I realized how much I loved this kind of feminine stuff and feeling pretty. Being an esthetician sounded interesting and had the promise of much better pay. If could make a living as a licensed esthetician, maybe one day I could have my own business.

To keep my promise to my mother, I also took college night classes studying education. But college was not my priority, so I focused on the certification program with business ownership as my goal. I had an entry-level point of view, but at least I had a vision for my future.

Within six months, I completed the course and received my certificate. I was almost free!

From a remote village to a big city, from tomboy to a young adult, I underwent many transitions. Beijing taught me that indoor plumbing, reliable electricity, refrigerators, and nice clothing were luxuries I could get used to. My active mind and adventurous personality fit perfectly with the modern, fast-paced vibe of city life. Living in Beijing opened my eyes and a doorway to my future. Seeing women wearing makeup and dressed to look beautiful introduced a new concept of beauty. Women in the village had no interest in such things. When the esthetician certificate made me realize I could make people beautiful, I began dreaming of beautiful things.

❋

The early morning San Francisco sun eased past the edge of the window shade to cast a thin sliver of light across my forehead. It was Saturday. My eyes popped open after a restless night, our final night in the apartment with Patrick and Sebrina.

How do I take care of a baby?

That thought played on an endless loop in my brain. Aside from tending our small herd of goats back in the village, I'd never taken care of anyone but myself. My mind wandered to a memory of me lying on the grass under the shade of a large tree to escape the summer heat while the goats grazed nearby. Goats were easy to take care of. But babies? A familiar knot of anxiety formed in my stomach.

Today we would move to the in-law apartment at Meghan and Jeff's exquisitely renovated three-story home. To me, it felt like a mansion. I'd never seen such a big house in my life. It sat on the highest hill in the neighborhood. Their large front porch faced a popular park where families, kids, and pets came to play and relax. It looked so perfect to me. A stunning view of the entire San Francisco downtown area was visible from our new front window.

The memory of walking into the small in-law studio for the first time remains vivid. A print of "The Kiss" painting by Klimt had been thoughtfully displayed in the living area. A beautiful fresh arrangement of yellow flowers and lilies on the bathroom counter filled the space with fragrance. Meghan had taken care to make it very welcoming. I will forever appreciate the opportunity and the sense of home they gave me.

One week before we moved in, Wei had taken me to meet the family and see the apartment.

"Please come in, Jing-Jing. It's wonderful to finally meet you." Meghan's belly hung large and low, signaling the impending birth of their baby. She shook my hand, then led Wei and me into the living room.

Jeff rose from his seat on the couch to greet us. "Why don't we show you the house, Jing-Jing?"

As Jeff and Meghan gave us the tour, I appreciated Meghan's effort to include me in the conversation, even though all I did was smile and nod. I quickly sensed a bond forming between this young mother and me, though not being able to communicate meant I had to feel my way through by using intuition. But kindness needs no translation.

I liked them right away. I walked away feeling a little relief and anxiously anticipating this new chapter in my life. The same way I had felt starting my new chapter in Beijing six short years prior.

CHAPTER 3

NEARING THE ONE-YEAR mark at the hotel in Beijing, I had long ago run out of patience for cleaning toilets. I spent my evenings in the hotel lobby pouring through help-wanted ads related to my newly earned certification as an esthetician. Most jobs required at least a year of experience, and I had none. But one night, I stumbled across an ad from a doctor who was opening a new spa across from the stock exchange in an affluent section of the city. The ad mentioned nothing about experience. I jumped at the opportunity, figuring I wouldn't mention my lack of experience if they didn't bring it up.

"Please come in. It's wonderful to meet you."

Dr. Xu met me at the future site of her new spa located in a one-story business plaza along one of the busiest streets in the city. Her handshake was firm. I guessed she was in her mid-forties. She exuded classic elegance and beauty with flawless hair and makeup complementing her high-fashion outfit. Being face to face with a polished professional who was considering hiring me made me suddenly self-conscious of my tomboy uniform of a tattered tee-shirt and jeans. Even my dress-up clothes weren't as nice as the outfits people wore in Beijing, and I'd never thought to dress up for an interview before.

Her status as a doctor was a big deal to me, but she seemed very casual about it. When we entered the unit that would be her new spa, I was a little shocked.

"It's kind of rough right now," she offered, noting the look on my face. "I will need your help with the renovations to get this started. I know it's a risk, but I am confident my medical background will be a tremendous advantage for the spa."

Dr. Xu explained that she recently quit her medical practice in a nearby city to start her business. She too was an outsider in Beijing. At the time, she was also divorcing her husband. Her determination to be independent felt very familiar, and her tenacity impressed me. We were kindred spirits.

"I will have no income until we get the spa open, but I can offer you a place to live as compensation." Her confidence inspired me to say *yes* without a second thought.

As you might imagine, my newest adventure did not go over very well back home.

"You are ruining your life!" Mother said.

I expected the heat of her anger to melt the phone right in my hand. My parents were frustrated with me because, once again, I had abandoned a secure job and a future with the hotel.

"You should be more stable," she continued. "I have nothing else to say."

The click that followed punctuated her statement.

Oh, Mother.

I let out a big sigh, realizing her disapproval still fueled my drive to prove myself.

Two weeks later, I moved my few worldly possessions into the basement of a high-rise building a few blocks away from where the new spa would open. The smell of stale mold hung in the damp cold air of the tiny room Dr. Xu and I shared. My dorm room at boarding school made this room feel like a closet. Three levels below the street, the basement was accessible only by one narrow stairway that opened to a central hallway leading to these small, windowless rooms. Looking back, I realize that a fire in the building would have meant certain death for those of us who rented rooms there.

Dr. Xu and I used boxes for furniture and simple mats on the floor as our beds. On a stack of boxes against one wall sat a lamp she had taken from her house before her ex-husband locked her out. That expensive lamp looked so out of place on that pile of boxes and plugged into a light fixture that dangled from the ceiling.

"We'll have to use the women's washroom on the second floor." Dr. Xu smiled at me, trying to soften the latest news about our already rough living arrangement. All basement tenants used those same facilities.

The conditions were not ideal, but better than conditions in my village, a detail I kept to myself. I focused on the vision of a new beginning, new learning, and a new adventure.

"I know this is really hard," Dr. Xu admitted, doing her best to encourage me. "I hope you'll hang on a little while. I know it will be worth it."

I understood why she had made no mention of prior experience in her ad: she just needed help.

Dr. Xu stood and turned out the lamp. Instant darkness consumed us. My eyes struggled to adjust, but there was nothing to see. As I lay on my mat, something inside me knew she was right. At the time, I didn't know that my intuition was telling me it would work out. I just thought, *If she can do it, if she can walk away from the many years invested to become a doctor, her medical career, and her home, then I have no excuse.*

I had only walked away from dirty toilets. The thread of intuition that was lurking in the background was beginning to reveal itself to me.

The hard work and long days of preparing the spa exhausted me in those first few months. I had used nearly all my savings from my hotel pay, so I could only scrape together enough to eat one meal a day. I was too proud to ask for help from my parents and didn't want to burden Dr. Xu. I dreamed of the day when I would stroll the city shopping for nice clothes like Dr. Xu's and prove to my parents they were wrong, that I could support myself and them.

The nearby ice cream shops carried dozens of flavors, sweet and creamy, and I longed to try them. It reminded me of the bicycle vendor and the simple ice cubes from another lifetime. Though much had changed, my drive for independence remained the same.

Strangely, I was happy. While biking through the city one morning, the warm wind played with my hair as I rode through the fragrant scents of fresh fruit in the vendor carts on the sidewalk. A powerful feeling of freedom filled me, even though I had nothing more in that moment than the rumbling song in my empty belly.

✳

"Do you have some tape I can borrow?" The young man who was opening a dry cleaning business in the adjacent unit once again stood in the doorway of the spa.

"I doubt he even needs tape," I mumbled to Dr. Xu. We both knew my annoyance was a facade. My heart raced whenever he stopped in. Dr. Xu winked at me and pointed to a box of supplies near the new reception counter.

Ming was tall, in his mid-twenties, muscular but lean, and a very handsome guy. In recent weeks, he made many excuses to ask for things he probably didn't need. His motives were obvious, and I was flattered. Since the age of six, I had been so busy forging my independence that I hadn't left much room in my life for boys. Most of my previous interactions took the form of defending my little brother by chasing off bullies with a stick. I took my self-appointed role of protector seriously. Nobody messed with my little brother.

Ming's visits gave us the chance to get to know each other a bit. His father was a senior leader in the military. They were a well-connected, wealthy family in Beijing. His parents had rented an apartment for him just down the street, and they were lending him startup funds for his business.

"Wow, that's fantastic. Good for you," I said when he told me.

I was mesmerized by his handsomeness and sweet nature. Even so, I wasn't about to invite him to visit the tiny basement room Dr. Xu and I shared. Instead, one day soon, I would welcome him to my new apartment.

In China, people born and raised in the big cities were snobby, looking down on people from small villages outside Beijing. They called us *DaGongMei*, a term for young Chinese migrant women. We were the women who moved to big cities in search of emancipation from the patriarchy and other social obligations we were pushed to accept.

"Can I take you to dinner sometime?" Ming asked.

He seemed sincere, and his entrepreneurial spirit enamored me. He didn't require the fiery independence Dr. Xu and I needed to get through each day. We were on our own, building a business from the ground up with no support. He had the luxury of support from his parents when he needed it. But his vision of success attracted me, much the same way that Dr. Xu's vision had drawn me in.

Ming's gorgeous body and handsome face were a bonus. I was so smitten that I chose to be open from the beginning about my background and my village life. In my mind, the risk was worth taking. He showed interest in my stories from back home and didn't seem to care about our class difference. Maybe it was my ability to will my way out of sticky situations, to do my best no matter what, that emboldened my risk-taking.

It didn't take me long to fall hard for my first real boyfriend. I truly believed we were in love. Brand-new threads of love and trust were weaving their way into my life, becoming beautifully entwined with the other threads I had picked up along the way.

✳

Nannying in San Francisco was the second job I took with no prior experience. Giving facials was not exactly life-threatening work, so learning on the job didn't affect a customer's safety. But the nannying job was different. I took it seriously, preparing by taking CPR and learning how to hold the baby properly. I repeated my mantra to do my best, no matter what. But my mantra didn't seem to fit this nanny situation. What if I messed up? Hurt her by mistake? Missed a sign that she needed help?

Crap, I'm afraid to touch her!

When Meghan went into labor, I thought they would stay in the hospital for a week like mothers did in China. I was surprised to see them return the next day with their brand-new baby in a car seat.

"Her name is Olivia," Meghan whispered as we stood in the master bedroom gazing at the newborn in the small bassinet.

Olivia looked so tiny and fragile. I fell in love with her on the spot.

With my English still nearly non-existent, I nodded a lot. Wei had translated important information to prepare me for the first days. Baby Olivia would sleep in the bassinet for the first six months, but I could use the changing table and rocking chair in the nursery as needed. I was to call 911 if there was an emergency.

What?

How would I explain what was wrong?

Wei worked with me on basic words like *help, baby, not breathing.* Despite my preparation, those words only terrified me more.

"I'll be back in two hours." Meghan put her arm around my shoulders and gave me a reassuring hug.

Can she see the terror on my face? Is it that obvious? And if it is, why isn't she terrified?

I nodded, a feeble smile giving me away. When the sound of the front door closing reached my ears, my breathing stopped. For the next hour, I stood in silence, my heart pounding like I was speed-climbing Mount Everest. Too afraid to leave her alone, I did nothing except watch baby Olivia sleep. I even stuck my pinkie finger in her nose to check if she was still breathing.

What if something happens if I leave the room? Thank God I don't have to pee. How do new parents sleep at night?

The days that followed became easier, but it took a while for my anxiety to fade. I began to feel like the only person I could communicate with was that baby. We understood each other, and our love began to deepen. She gave me relief from having to figure out the right words. We didn't have to talk. Baby Olivia didn't care what language I spoke. She smiled at everything I said.

I loved to make the baby giggle. I didn't want her just laying around, so as she grew, I constantly interacted with her—playing, talking, and bouncing her.

Meghan hugged me every day to show her gratitude. She didn't understand that Asian people don't hug. We just don't. Hugging is a western custom. I never exchanged hugs with my parents as a child or young adult. Even now, when they come to the US to visit, it is still awkward to hug them, although I've become a big hugger when greeting people I care about. Meghan was the first person to introduce me to a hug as a sign of affection and appreciation, one of many things she taught me. I wanted the affectionate part of this culture for my life and my family. The open communication and ability to express your love for someone felt right, strengthening my thread of love in a new way I guess I was learning more than a new language. I was learning how to be American.

❋

Wanting to help, to do my part, to contribute, are traits that were baked into me at birth. Sitting still never felt right. Sneaking back to the kitchen of our small single-story house one night, I set the oil lamps ablaze and made the best tomato egg-drop soup ever. At least, at eight years old, I thought it was the best ever. I knew my family was hungry from working in the fields, and I wanted to surprise them. The real surprise was discovering my love of cooking. It gave me a way to contribute but also a way to show my worth and my love.

A few weeks into my nanny job, I felt the itch to do something different, anything beyond just watching the baby sleep. I wanted to make good on the hours Meghan and Jeff were exchanging for the in-law apartment. I used some of the idle time to study English and feed my obsession with cooking shows on PBS. The shows really helped with my English. But Meghan and Jeff had been so generous that it didn't seem fair for me to just watch TV.

Cleaning toilets and mopping floors were areas of expertise for me, but that work didn't need to be done every day. I washed dishes and folded any laundry I found. I just wasn't sure where to put it away. One morning, I spotted an enormous pile of clothing on the floor in their laundry room.

Why don't I wash the laundry? I have experience from my days running the dry cleaning business. How hard could it be?

I had my answer not long after I dumped a little too much bleach into a load that didn't really need it. What a mess I made! I destroyed their clothing. Every last piece of that load was ruined.

I know better than this! I fumed.

For some reason, all the instructions on the cleaning supplies made me feel dizzy. I did my best to read the labels and carefully followed directions based on my reading skills in English and comprehension of cleaning supplies. It should have been easy for me. Instead, it knocked my confidence to the ground.

Do I have to learn everything all over again?

Frustration and overwhelm battled it out in my head. When Meghan got home, I felt like a guilty dog sulking in the corner for chewing on the couch. I motioned for Meghan to follow me to the laundry room.

"Oh, no! What happened, Jing-Jing?" Meghan giggled as she lifted shirts, socks, and underwear that now looked like really bad tie-dye out of the basket.

You think this is funny?

I felt like a fool. I managed to communicate to Meghan that I would use my work hours to pay for the damage I caused.

"I love that you wanted to help, Jing." She smiled her warm, forgiving smile and dismissed my offer to pay. "Why don't I show you how to do the laundry? That would be a great help to me."

She would be an amazing mother, and I would be forever grateful.

Sometimes Meghan and Jeff took me with them to events and gatherings, but I couldn't socialize. I felt invisible and didn't like it at all. The loneliness and uncomfortable situations drained my confidence.

After Olivia's first birthday, they decided to vacation in Hawaii and asked us to come with them so I could take care of her there. Wei and I didn't have much money because neither of us had paying jobs. We were so worried about how we would pay for our expenses.

I think Meghan read my thoughts from the look on my face when she invited us.

"We'll take care of everything, Jing," she said. "We're renting a villa so we can cook and eat in."

Wei and I still calculated every penny we spent. We stuffed our suitcases with so many packages of ramen that they bulged. We even packed a cabbage, but airport staff discovered it, so we had to throw it out. Meghan and Jeff were so generous to us on the trip, but it went against my nature to rely on them. Gratitude and awkwardness jumbled together inside me the entire time.

In the year and a half that I nannied for them, my English improved greatly. The exposure to many different interactions expanded my understanding and use of the language. Being their nanny was more than just a job. But we were not peers, and I remained sensitive to our differences. I lacked a full sense of confidence. I still doubted myself because of the language barrier. I often wondered how I could survive in this place, in this country. But remembering that we planned to return to China soon, and knowing we would live such a good life there, gave me something to look forward to.

Learning a new language taught me a deeper lesson. I came to understand that I have to be real about myself, not take myself too seriously, and embrace my learning curve. If I am uncomfortable, I will make other people nervous. I learned to accept the fact that some people will accept me, and some will not. I eventually chose to take the viewpoint that it's not my problem; it is their problem. I believe it is okay to be awkward while I am learning. Self-confidence was a thread I would need to weave into my life with intention, continuing to strengthen it over and over again.

Meghan and Jeff were incredibly gracious and helpful to me while I cared for baby Olivia. I learned about culture, family life, and how to speak my own form of "Jinglish" from this beautiful family. They were a bright spot throughout this challenging season of my life. Their kindness reminded me of my time with Dr. Xu.

✳

Despite the busy schedule and challenges of getting the spa ready, Dr. Xu's smile grew brighter as we drew closer to welcoming the first customer.

"Are you excited about opening day?" she asked.

Because we were developing a deep trust in each other, I was brutally honest with her. "Yes! I'm ready to make money," I replied.

Dr. Xu laughed. "Me too!" We were both tired of being hungry cellar dwellers. Dr. Xu inspired me. Even though she was my boss, we were both strangers in a strange city, and we bonded over our common situation of being single with nothing and no one to help us. If she became successful, I would become successful too. I put 100 percent into helping her, and she saw my dedication.

We never mentioned the term "mentor" in all the time we worked together. I'm not sure I knew what it meant back then. But I watched carefully, observing her decision-making style and tenacity to fight for better prices to keep costs down. I watched how she managed the advertising, the bookkeeping, and how she built relationships with suppliers and neighboring business owners. I watched her struggle. I watched as she pretended everything was okay. She almost cried a few times, but she held back the tears, trying not to show her concern.

During the build-out, Dr. Xu put signage on the front of the spa. To do so, she needed to obtain local government approval, but the process for doing so was not very clear. The snobby locals treated outsiders differently and made it very difficult for her. She had to work twice as hard to complete this simple task.

I sensed her frustration, but she just dealt with whatever came her way. I watched as she meticulously fixed her long hair and makeup and dressed in a smart-looking outfit, no matter what was happening in the business. I absorbed it all.

Writing this book meant taking a close look at my time with Dr. Xu and how much that experience impacted me. Dr. Xu's determination rubbed off. It's where I picked up threads of determination and courage and began to see their importance in the tapestry I was weaving. I recognized how she did it, and I began to do it too. Thinking about her gave me strength when I needed it. Her determination and rebellious spirit strengthened mine and carried me through many of my own challenges. They served as my bulletproof vest, allowing me to not care what others thought of me.

Dr. Xu was not the only strong woman I learned from. I got strength, competitiveness, and determination from my hardworking mother. She never stopped. Now, every time I encounter an obstacle, no matter how large, I look for what it can teach me to become better and stronger. Just like the strong women I learned from; I will find a way.

The business boomed from the day we opened. I handled booking appointments and mostly did facials because I wasn't very skilled at makeup, and the idea of hair removal made me cringe. Each evening of that first week, we discussed the advantages of our location across from the stock exchange and next to the dry cleaners. We talked about the power of her medical background, which gave her instant credibility with new customers.

"You made a lot of money this week . . ." My tired mind wandered through the craziness of all that had happened as I lay on my mat in our tiny room. "And we booked customer appointments for the next month!" I couldn't contain my amazement.

"No, Jing-Jing. *We* made a lot of money." Dr. Xu reached across her mat to hand me the largest stack of cash I'd ever seen. "Thank you for sticking with me through all of this."

"Wow," was all that came out of my mouth.

She handed that money to *me*, the tomboy with no experience. She truly appreciated me. Her recognition of my contribution to the business meant the world to me. Honestly, I was really happy that she made it through the launch of her business. She treated me as an equal and mentored me. She raised my salary as soon as she could, which allowed me to move out to my own place. I was happy even without a raise because I learned so much from her. But it was a thrill to move from that dingy basement to my first apartment in Beijing.

I upgraded to a studio-style room above ground with a single window and a small countertop cabinet with a gas burner, which meant I could cook for myself. I still shared a bathroom and shower, but it didn't matter. I had become independent. And I had become a regular at a nearby ice cream shop. Pure heaven.

Over the next year, Dr. Xu continued to pay me with large stacks of cash. I became her confidante, her right hand helping to manage the business. All the while, I continued to absorb her business and fashion sense. She unknowingly helped me transform from a small village tomboy into a fashionable young woman and aspiring entrepreneur. I made the most money I'd ever made in my life, and the experience cemented the money-entrepreneur connection in my mind. I was hooked. It set me up perfectly for my first entrepreneurial adventure.

Can you guess what business I got into?

Dry cleaning, of course.

CHAPTER 4

MING, MY HANDSOME dry-cleaning boyfriend, and I had been dating for a little over a year. Both the spa and his business enjoyed steady growth during that time, and we talked about business often.

One evening over dinner, he surprised me by saying, "I think you should be in business with me. I could really use your help to expand."

My brain latched onto the word *expand*, sending it into overdrive. Clearly, the location across from the stock exchange worked well for his business too. Our conversation that night lit a new fire in me. I envisioned myself running the largest dry-cleaning business in Beijing with multiple locations, maybe expanding into linen service for hotels and restaurants. I saw no limit to the possibilities, so in my classic cut-to-the-chase manner, I said *yes*.

Plus, I was more than a little in love.

Dr. Xu and I had hired a full staff which she could manage by herself, and her business had become very stable. I knew she would continue to do well without me.

"It sounds like a terrific opportunity." Dr. Xu's smile filled her face with warmth. "I know you will be successful. And I will always be grateful for the help you gave me."

I had learned so much from her. It was important to me that we parted as friends.

Within a few weeks of that conversation, I took over running the dry-cleaning shop. My responsibilities were hiring, managing the business and finances, and planning to scale it. My ads and promotions brought in even more customers. I endured many sleepless nights to make sure the work got finished. Once I'm into something, I give it 100 percent effort.

"I found a great two-bedroom apartment two blocks away." When Ming suggested we move in together, my heart sang at the opportunity to give 100 percent effort to love. We were crazy about each other. I never realized that my life could be so good.

Within a few months, Ming began losing interest in dry cleaning and spent little time at the shop, but I was fully engaged in growing the business. Stocks and investing had become his focus, so I didn't think much about his disinterest. One morning, he walked into the shop with a well-dressed middle-aged couple.

"I want you to meet my parents." Ming wore a nervous smile as I came from behind the counter to greet them. He had told his parents I came from the village. I felt their disapproval as they looked down to assess me. I saw they cared more about my lower-class background than the hard work I did to build their son's business.

Ming went to the back of the shop to get drinks for them, leaving us alone. After several minutes of awkward silence, his father finally spoke.

"You are not a match for our son. He will have a much better future with a wife who is a lawyer or a doctor."

His words pierced me like the blade of a *dao*.

Then his mother spoke up. "I beg you to leave him. He is our only son."

"Yes," his father said. "We set up some dates for him, and he went to each of them willingly."

"What?" My voice trembled from shock.

"Father!" Ming came back just in time to hear the last part of our conversation.

I felt belittled and betrayed, that I was somehow less than they were. I didn't cry often back then, but I blinked back tears as he ushered them out of the shop.

Memories of my fourth-grade trip to Beijing rushed into my mind along with the feeling of being "less than." Our clothing and lifestyle were so glaringly different from the sophistication of city people. But this time was much worse. Hurt and anger filled me. I felt like I was not enough. I felt disrespected, devalued, and betrayed. The two people looking down on me were Mings's parents, sending my emotions into a tumble of conflict. Their actions, all three of them, felt very cowardly to me.

My first taste of betrayal was bitter. It was a very dramatic time in my life. It is not uncommon for young people to break up and get back together over and over, but I sensed this would not be the case with Ming and me.

Ming apologized and blamed his parents, insisting they pushed him to date the women they had arranged for him. In Beijing, when people looked down on me, I was determined to make myself better, to show them my worth. *I don't need you* would become stuck on replay in my head.

I hated not being considered an equal because I am not "less than" them. I had value and worth, but they tried to make me feel otherwise. I wouldn't let anyone define who I was. But this time, it was the parents of the man I loved. This time, it was personal.

❋

My love for Ming and my commitment to the business vision we shared made a crazy, powerful combination. The flame of that fire engulfed my whole person. At twenty-four, it was my first experience with something so deep and emotional.

Ming ignored his parents for the first half of our relationship. We were so in love that he didn't care what they thought. But as time went on, their influence affected him. I confronted Ming about the dates, and he admitted to complying with his parents. He worried their health might suffer if he didn't do what they told him to do. This revelation touched off a season of arguments. Our constant arguing was destructive and stressful. While I understood the pressure he was under, the breakdown in our communication created more resentment, anger, and distrust.

"I'm sorry, Jing-Jing, but I want to break up," he finally said. "This isn't what I want."

His words kicked me so hard in the gut I couldn't breathe.

"But . . ." My eyes locked on him, searching for an answer.

Clearly, he had already made his decision, and it was final. With one short sentence, he dismantled my entire life and future. Adding to my agony, he told me he wanted to sell the business. I was making crazy money, even more than at the spa, but now I was being forced to break up with my entrepreneurial vision as well as my boyfriend. The situation delivered a major, devastating blow. Overnight, the threads of love and trust had reached their breaking point.

In the two-and-a-half years we were together, I proved to my parents and family that my way of life was stable, that I could make money. I sent money home instead of expecting them to support me. I proved that my decisions of opting for night college, leaving the village and the hotel, and taking risks, could pay off. My choices were transforming into the life I always envisioned. But now, this beautiful season of experiences with my first real boyfriend and my first real business partnership ended with my first breakup.

I entered a new season: my first dance with depression. I had never experienced that kind of heartache and emotional pain. I was lost.

As depression set in, I could only think about getting far away to clear my head. I withdrew from the world, spending most of my time alone. An endless loop of questions ran through my brain. *Am I good enough? Am I really capable of being a life partner? A business owner?*

I had always fought hard to prove I was good enough to other people. Ming's parents activated a sense of less-than in me, but this time, I didn't question other people's opinion, I questioned my own. Depression had me fighting hard to believe I was good enough. Between the business, the apartment, and our relationship, our lives had become so intertwined that it took months to make a clean break. Fortunately, my frugalness, saving habits, and investments meant I could support myself during this transition.

But before this season ended, I added two more first experiences to my repertoire. And they weren't pretty. The good and bad news was they happened at the same time. I finally moved to a tiny apartment of my own, and that first night was pretty rough. The pain had become so unbearable that I just wanted to escape. I went to a nearby liquor store.

"What kind of Baijiu tastes good?" I asked the shopkeeper. (Baijiu is a type of whiskey.)

"Here. You will like Erguotou." The shopkeeper, who reminded me of my father, plunked a bottle down on the counter between us. For a fleeting moment, I wondered what my father would say if he saw me.

You are ruining your life! His voice echoed loud and clear in my head.

"No. Give me the bigger bottle," I said, having no idea what I was doing. Alcohol never appeared in our house. If my parents drank, they hid it very well. I'd seen drunks in the village but had a limited understanding of how they achieved that state of being.

"And I'll take a pack of cigarettes too," I added.

The shopkeeper's scowl trumpeted his disapproval. I apparently didn't look or smell anything like his regular customers.

It was dark by the time I returned to my silent little apartment with a paper bag of sins. I grabbed a glass from the cabinet and set everything up on a small end table in the living room. In keeping with my nightly routine, I flopped into an exasperated lump on the couch and let out a deep sigh. I started gulping shots of Erguotou, but I don't recall actually liking the drink. However, that didn't stop me from needing to hold on to the walls during trips to the bathroom.

This isn't working that well. Time to numb myself with cigarettes.

Not sure where I got the idea that cigarettes had a numbing effect, but I was in full what-the-hell mode. I smoked the entire pack, one after another, creating a thick cloud that seemed to fill the entire apartment.

My next attempt to stand was downright ugly. My head spun and my eyes flipped back into my skull. I crawled on hands and knees to the bathroom, where my stomach lost its ability to manage the toxic mix in my system.

Somewhere in the haze of my excess, I wondered why my peers did this kind of thing every weekend. I realized this behavior was not me. At least I could say that I did it once. But my evening of excess solved nothing. I got up the next morning with a massive hangover and stuck in the same damn hole I had been in the day before.

How stupid. This season is over. I'm moving on.

✳

Losing everything that mattered brought me to a low point that turned out to be a blessing. Being knocked down was an excellent teacher. I absorbed two important lessons in that season. First, I learned about survival. Even though the pain and heartache were unbearable, I would be okay. I learned that I would survive starting my life over again. I could cry at night and still be productive the next day. Letting go of the past proved horribly difficult, but it taught me to look forward and cope. Journaling became my way to cope and get my feelings out. I remember letting my teardrops land on a blank page of my journal. Then I took my pen and captured each one in its own cloud. Second, I discovered that business was great medicine for all that pain, far better than booze and cigarettes. This experience tested my life tapestry for the first time. Strong threads of determination and courage made up for strained threads of love and trust, giving me a sense of support at just the right moment.

The idea of getting another job never crossed my mind. Once again, I found myself looking through the newspaper each day to see what might catch my interest. This time, an ad for a singles dating service pulled me in. I'd been alone long enough.

I wonder what that's like. I'll try it. Why not?

"What are you interested in?" Mei, the general manager of the dating service, had asked me to come to the office to interview me for my profile. She was only a few years older than me, and I wondered if she took the job to meet men.

Smart way to be first in line.

"I'm an entrepreneur. I love the challenge of starting a business," I replied, sparking a lively exchange of ideas.

"I'm going to introduce you to Hua. She registered here too, and she loves business. We should meet for dinner," Mei said.

Our first meeting two weeks later felt electric. Mei, Hua, and I shared a love for thinking big and taking risks. It felt invigorating to be with like-minded women. That evening breathed life back into me.

"Just between us," Mei leaned in and lowered her voice, "I've been thinking about starting a dating service for executive women."

"I wonder what else we could do for women . . ." My mind was already speeding through ideas to improve what I thought could be the best part: gatherings and outings.

As if Mei read my mind, she said, "We are thinking about starting a membership club focused on professional single women. Would you like to join us?"

We believed we could create a successful women-focused business model, which no one else was doing. The cultural expectation for women to marry young and have a family made it difficult for successful "older" career women in their thirties and forties—called "leftovers"—to find partners. As a rather new business approach at that time, we could meet that need without competing with the existing businesses for singles.

I longed to be around successful friends. At twenty-five, I was the youngest of the three of us. My two partners were thirty-something and forty-something. Our entrepreneurial adventure took off. We shared ownership and responsibilities as business partners. We created a hybrid membership and dating model, hosting outings at different locations around the city, day trips, and weekend getaways. It was so different from my other businesses! We had so much fun that we didn't really care that the business wasn't making much money. Membership grew fast, and we even invited the owner of the dating service that brought us together to join. She did!

I considered my first business partnership to be a success. I loved who I worked with and the experience of mutual partnership. There weren't many women running businesses back then. Working with and learning from women felt inspiring; I was drawn to the resilience and determination I saw in them. I knew I wanted the beautiful thread of friendship woven into my life.

During our two-year run, the business never became financially successful, but we had fun and got to date a few nice guys too. I dated one guy who had a beautiful convertible sports car. After dinner out one evening, he let me drive it. Instead of thinking that I could marry him and get to drive it all the time, as many women might, I thought, *One day, I'm going to buy myself one of these.*

The events and socializing were fun, but part of my life still felt empty. A few of the men I dated were nice, but most were showy and arrogant, and I never found a deeper connection with any of them.

✳

Hua invited me to a private party that her friend, Lingyun, was hosting, and I was eager to attend. Our business gave us the opportunity to date and have fun experiences with new people, but I hadn't met anyone who seemed to be a fit for me. At twenty-six, I didn't even know what I wanted. My broken heart experience was two years behind me, but the sting lingered, keeping me cautious. Yet I yearned for companionship.

Lingyun's condo was beautiful, overlooking the city from the eighth floor of a high-rise near the financial district. An eclectic mix of guests attended the party: lawyers, stockbrokers, a few Beijing socialites and artists, and entrepreneurs like me and Hua. The beige walls of the condo made the perfect backdrop for his expansive collection of Tibetan art.

"You've discovered my favorite. It's a thangka by a Tibetan Buddhist monk painted on cotton, depicting the five Wisdom Kings." A young man stopped and turned shoulder to shoulder with me to admire the painting. He was not flashy or particularly handsome like the other men in the room. "Lingyun only hangs them when he's having a party."

"It's exquisite." I turned to smile at him and offered a handshake. "I'm Jing."

"I'm Wei. Nice to meet you. Jing means calm and peaceful. Is that fitting for you?"

"Ha-ha! Not at all!" We laughed easily together.

My intuition told me he was a kind person. It was right. After an engaging conversation about the artwork, Wei and I made our way to a sofa in the living room, captive in our own little world, oblivious to the other guests as the hours flew by. His intelligence, love for the arts, and humble nature drew me in. An avid reader, he loved topics like history, science, art, and entertainment. Wei had long, silky hair that he kept in a loose ponytail neatly secured at the base of his neck. He was a true Renaissance man, a unique trait among the men I'd been dating. Most of them pretended to be smart, but for Wei, there was no hiding it.

"I'm staying with Lingyun while I apply for my visa," he said. "It has taken me three times, but I am hopeful they will approve it this time. I was accepted to a university in San Francisco to study law."

In the week that followed that party, Wei and I spent time together or talked on the phone every day.

"My visa got approved!" Wei told me in a jumble of excitement and nerves. He had insisted I come to the condo so he could share the news. We sat on the same sofa where we spent hours the weekend before.

He turned to face me. "Jing, I've never met a girl who has a big heart like you do. You give me strength and confidence that no one ever has. Will you marry me?"

Can you guess how the risk-taking Jing responded?

❋

Six months before Wei's proposal, I had moved my parents and my brother to an apartment in Beijing. My parents no longer questioned my business pursuits. We simply didn't talk much about my career or my life anymore. I preferred it that way. Instead, we focused on the new construction materials business I was helping them start. My years and experiences in Beijing strengthened my intuition thread, and I learned to listen and trust it. When something felt right, I jumped at the opportunity. And so it was with the construction materials business and with Wei. Both were taking off, so I had to tell my parents about our impending marriage and move. No matter where we ended up, I knew it would be great to marry Wei. He planned to stay in the US for two years, then return to Beijing and start his own law firm.

We walked into my parents' apartment, and I cut right to the chase. "Hello. I'm excited to introduce my fiancée, Wei." He had forgotten to tuck his ponytail into the back of his shirt, and the long strands slid over his shoulder when he bent down to greet them. My parents were not impressed.

"What?" Mother gasped. My father sat stone-faced on the couch, and my brother became wide-eyed and silent.

"We've been dating for about a year now." I had lied to them about the struggles and living in the basement with Dr. Xu, but those were mostly little white lies to keep them from worrying and pestering me. I had never delivered a lie quite this bold. "I didn't want to mention it until the right time. And now we are moving."

We did not plan out our fake story, and neither of us were comfortable lying, but I knew the fact that Wei and I had just met would not sit well.

"Wei brought you a present. Look!" Wei placed the large box containing a microwave oven on the coffee table in front of them. He tried to be as gracious as possible. My parents were as cold as stone. To be fair, I had prepared him for it. And my parents reacted as anyone would to the bombshells I dropped.

"Moving?" Mother struggled to take it all in.

We spent the next hour explaining our reasoning for getting married and Wei's opportunity to study in the US.

"I am very concerned about you leaving the country, Jing-Jing." Mother was still adjusting to life in the city. She had never left China and could only imagine the worst of the US.

"Well, you know, many people follow their dream of going to the US because they believe they can have an adventure in a new world and make a lot of money," I said.

Mother waved her hand, dismissing the popular idea. I don't think she believed me or my reasoning, but I couldn't be sure. Our communication had always been so bad. I never told them my struggles, ever. I didn't like to worry them, and I didn't want their pushback.

The next few months flew by in a whirlwind. We had a small informal ceremony with just a few friends and our families in attendance. Everything happened quickly, so there was no elaborate wedding gown for me, even though I dreamed of wearing one. I had used my savings to buy a condominium in Beijing for my family and helped them move. I took comfort in knowing they would be fine no matter what happened to the construction materials business while I was away. In my role as family protector, moving them to Beijing met an important goal and strengthen my family thread. I wanted to give them a better life.

✳

"I will see you soon." Wei stopped at the gate to wave goodbye, then boarded his plane for San Francisco.

Watching him leave shifted my mind into overdrive. *What would the US be like? What would our marriage be like? Would my parents and brother be okay without me here to take care of them?* That moment tugged on my thread of trust in a different way, testing its strength.

Moving from the village to Beijing had been a big step. At first, I felt out of place and overwhelmed, but I kept moving forward. I did my best, no matter what. Leaving China for the US presented an entirely different challenge level. It opened a much bigger world to me, sparking excitement mixed with anxiety. After Wei left, I applied for a companion visa and took a couple of English classes in a feeble attempt to prepare for life in the US.

But nothing could prepare me for the new world I was about to experience.

CHAPTER 5

WEI GRADUATED from law school with a concentration in patent law. Now we could follow our plan to move back to China, a secret relief for me. After two years in the US, I felt ready to go home. I missed my former life of business adventures, my social circle, and being there to take care of my family.

"I want to sit for the California Bar Exam before we leave the country," Wei announced.

"Do you think you can pass it?" I asked.

"Not sure. But it's worth trying. It will help us make our $200,000," Wei reminded me. "Then we will be rich."

During our two years in San Francisco, we talked often about making lots of money here and then moving back to China. The favorable exchange back to RMB would've converted to almost two million RMB, making us millionaires in China. The thought of such an enormous sum excited both of us. That number stuck with me. We wanted the success and sense of security we believed it would provide.

Our naivete still makes me smile. Wei did not pass the test on his first try, but we were convinced it was worth trying again. He was thrilled when he met success the second time. Not long after, he found a law firm in New York City that agreed to sponsor his work visa.

"I really want to get some experience here in the US. I'm going to take the job," Wei said.

My heart sank. I wanted to support my husband in his career, but I yearned to go back to Beijing as we had planned. Wei believed he would have great opportunities and more autonomy in the US. He was half right; a level of autonomy was afforded to everyone. His starting salary at the law firm was low by New York City standards but it allowed us to stay.

I admired Wei so much for his knowledge, all that he taught me about art, and his worldliness. As two people dropped into a strange world, we survived by working together. Our relationship held strong. But during the first two years, I managed to lose myself in our relationship. My identity had been absorbed into our marriage, until who I was became almost undetectable. I thought returning to China would mean returning to the real me.

Now what do I do?

The day we packed our meager belongings and boarded a plane for New York, my stomach knotted. The city held promise for us, but I would miss the friends we made during our time in San Francisco. I would likely never see baby Olivia again.

As the plane taxied, my mind raced. I had no friends, no job. My ability to stay in the US still depended upon my companion visa, and my Jinglish was still shaky.

What will my future be like? How can I help us reach our goal?

I closed my eyes as the plane slipped through the thick gray cloud deck. I felt the uncertainty of this move, but I looked forward to seeing New York City because I'd heard it was the center of fashion.

New everything, all over again. A heavy sigh escaped my lips.

✳

I slid across the back seat of the taxi while Wei loaded our bags into the trunk. The mix of masculine body odor, exhaust fumes, and stale cigarette smoke overwhelmed me. My stomach flipped. Our taxi driver, a young man of Indian descent, swerved, accelerated, and braked hard through the crowded streets, adding to my nausea. His limited knowledge of English was oddly comforting.

Maybe my Jinglish isn't so bad.

New York City felt big and busy, reminding me of Beijing and my longing for home.

The tiny apartment we moved to sat on the southern border of New York City's Chinatown near the Supreme Court Building, just five blocks away from the World Trade Center and Twin Towers. Our studio apartment on the tenth floor had only one window, and it faced the exterior wall of the building next door. The buildings were so close I could touch that wall if I leaned out, which meant our apartment received no meaningful daylight. It reminded me of the basement room I had once shared with Dr. Xu.

Maybe that's a good sign?

Nearly three years of marriage and we finally had the first place of our own. It made me so happy. Now we could settle into being us and following our own path. We had rooftop access and usually had the area to ourselves because none of the other residents wanted to deal with the dirt and soot. We cleaned a corner and set up two chairs to make it our oasis. The two of us enjoyed being on the roof on hot summer evenings, far above the noise and craziness of the streets.

"This congee tastes like home." I filled my belly with the goodness and leaned my head on Wei's shoulder. Having real Chinese food in my stomach helped quell homesickness. Connecting with him and working to build our life together felt really wonderful. That rooftop became one of my happy places.

✳

"I'm going to Washington, D.C.!" I announced one evening.

My companion visa limited my ability to work, but my desire to help us reach our goals drove me to find whatever work I could get. Scanning the newspaper, I spotted an ad for a travel agency in Chinatown seeking Chinese-speaking tour guides.

Once again, I thought, *Why not me? I can do that.*

Knowing very little about America's capital didn't seem to matter.

They sent me on a bus to Washington to see how I did and to help me learn the job.

"How did it go?" Wei greeted me at the door upon my return, doing his best to hide his concern but clearly relieved to see that I had found my way back. My Jinglish was still developing, and Washington was a long way from New York City.

"Eh. It was okay." I slumped onto the living room sofa and sighed, exhausted from an endless day of travel. "They paid me in cash, but not very well. Only forty dollars."

The next thing Wei said surprised me: "It's not your passion." His smile warmed my soul.

"Maybe I should go back to school for something . . ."

"Okay, but don't go to school just to get a job," he cautioned. "Do something you love."

I loved running businesses but getting into an industry I also loved had never occurred to me before that moment. I had always worked to make money, which served me well back in China. The idea of combining two things I love, entrepreneurship and my passion, would change my life forever. At age twenty-eight, I discovered the thread of passion.

But can I make money doing something I love? And what would I love to do?

❄

Despite our meager income, Wei was very supportive and encouraged me to pursue what I enjoyed. I spent the next week daydreaming and cooking. Our apartment's kitchen was tiny, but I cooked up a storm out of that little room.

Food connects people, and my love of cooking and entertaining had blossomed in San Francisco. We sometimes hosted Wei's classmates for dinner, giving me the opportunity to explore my culinary curiosity. In New York, we expanded our friend circle through dinner gatherings. I learned to go shopping at the end of the day, before the food stands closed, when the groceries were discounted. I'd make *shalambao* and steamed Chinese buns. Soup dumplings were another favorite. I'd prepare the soup dumplings from scratch. I made a filling of crab eggs, ginger, soy sauce, and chicken broth. After mixing a dough of flour and water, I'd roll and fill each wrapper. The dumplings were steamed until cooked through and the soup inside became hot and savory. Soup dumplings were an all-day project.

I made so many recipes in that little kitchen. Inspiration from the PBS cooking shows came to life in my dark little apartment. I picked up the thread of passion, examining it closely.

Should I go to culinary school?

It was an interesting option, but concern that my enjoyment would fade if I worked full-time in the restaurant industry quickly put an end to that question. Feeding family and friends filled me with a joy I didn't want to lose.

One beautiful late summer weekend, something truly magical happened in Central Park. There, amidst the tranquil beauty of the park, I happened upon a wedding. It felt as though the universe had orchestrated the perfect scene, and I was fortunate enough to be a spectator. As I watched the bride gracefully glide down the aisle in her wedding dress, my heart skipped a beat. She wore a spectacular dress, something out of a fairy tale, and the vision entranced me. I had always been a sucker for a good love story, and that dress represented the ultimate love story in fabric form. The dress wrapped the bride in a cocoon of pure elegance and romance. I couldn't tear my eyes away.

Maybe someday I can have a piece of that magic for myself.

Most girls dream of their wedding day, and I was no different. But when Wei and I married, I didn't have the opportunity to wear a formal wedding dress. The allure of flowing fabrics, intricate lace, and the magic of being transformed into a bride remained a distant dream.

Back in our little apartment, I searched online to learn more about wedding dresses. When I stumbled upon Vera Wang's breathtaking collection, I was instantly drawn to Vera and the stories about her clientele. From Mariah Carey (who married Tommy Mottola in 1993) to Spice Girl Victoria Beckham (who married soccer heartthrob David

Beckham in 1999), the women who chose Vera's gowns for their nuptials wanted to express their own unique styles and personalities. Vera didn't just design dresses; she created experiences. She invited brides to explore their own creativity, embrace their individuality, and celebrate who they truly were on one of the most important days of their lives.

But it was more than the elegance of her designs and the stories. Vera's entrepreneurial spirit and her background lit a spark in me. A fellow Asian woman who embarked on her fashion journey at age forty, Vera embodied creativity and passion, and she stirred the same in me.

If she can bring her visions to life in the world of fashion, why can't I?

And so, with a heart full of ambition and my eyes set on the horizon, I decided that fashion would be the canvas for my story. I couldn't wait to share my discovery with Wei.

He hadn't even closed the door to our apartment after work that day before I barraged him with my thoughts.

"I saw this wedding in the park today. It got me thinking, so I did some research online. Wedding fashion is amazing. I think I want to get into fashion, but I have no training or experience. I don't think I'm qualified yet, but—"

Wei's eyes sparkled with enthusiasm. "Jing, look at you. I haven't seen you this excited in years." He had always loved the arts, design, and fashion, so the idea thrilled him too. "If this is your passion, then do it."

His support meant the world to me. I will always be grateful to him for urging me to follow this path. Vera's story, which I still hold dear after all these years, was the spark that ignited my dreams. Vera became my North Star.

The more I sat with the idea, imagining how this thread of passion would feel woven into my life, the stronger my desire grew. I envisioned becoming a fashion designer.

One day, I will have my own runway show in New York.

But I had zero experience or training, and I didn't know if I even had a creative side. Once again, others would doubt my choice. I decided to put myself first, and my decision was based on joy.

The first task on my journey to becoming a fashion designer was a tall order: find an affordable nearby school that would accept me. The neighborhood library supplied all the tools I needed for my search. To my delight, I discovered the State University of New York had a school in the heart of the city dedicated to fashion. The Fashion Institute of Technology, or FIT for short, had a terrific reputation and met most of my requirements.

On a beautiful September evening, Wei and I strolled the sidewalk along Battery Park, discussing my discovery. We often walked through the neighborhood looking for inexpensive restaurants and talking about our day.

"I will have to apply right away. Fall semester classes are starting next week." I could barely contain my excitement.

"And when you become a fashion designer and we have money, I will take you *there*." Wei pointed to Windows on the World, the restaurant on the 107th floor of the World Trade Center. Since we moved to New York City Wei dreamed of dining there. Doing so would mean we reached our goal, that we were rich, successful, and secure.

I loved that Wei was a dreamer and a visionary. We had such big plans, and they filled me with hope for the future.

The next morning, the world and our lives changed forever. I was busy in our little kitchen when a massive explosion erupted—something much louder than typical city noise. Wei was watching the news when a breaking news report told us a plane had flown into one of the Twin Towers. Wei and I went into the street to watch what was happening. A crowd had gathered on a nearby street corner, pointing at the towers only five blocks away, but we could not see what was going on.

I heard the second plane hit the second tower with the same massive boom that had drawn us onto the street. The crowd gasped. Glass shattered. Metal groaned against metal. So terribly loud. Then, without warning, the first tower crumbled to the ground. Amidst the horrific sounds of destruction, people gasped and shouted, "Oh my God, oh my God . . ." Police shouted, telling the crowds to run, and people barreled toward us. In an instant, thick dust and smoke plumes filled the streets. We couldn't see the sky.

Wei and I ran north amidst a sea of people. We turned the corner toward the East River, only to see the Brooklyn Bridge flooded with people running to escape Manhattan. I was sure the bridge would collapse from the weight of so many people. No one seemed to know where they were going, and strangely, no one cried. We were all too shocked to cry. I think we all feared the world was ending. As we crossed the bridge, I looked at the sky and wondered if another plane would come. With so much emotional overwhelm, we didn't know what to think.

It was the most surreal moment of my life and by far the most horrible experience I would ever endure. Thick dust gathered in our shoes, hair, and lungs. The non-stop wail of sirens punctuated the eerie absence of traffic, horns, and people. It seemed other-worldly, as though we were walking through the scene of a horror movie.

Late in the day, we returned to our apartment to see if we could get in. Exhausted and relieved, we climbed the stairs to our little apartment. A thick layer of dust completely covered our only window, but in the center of all the chaos, our apartment felt safe.

We felt so broken for all the people who lost their lives that day, just a few blocks away. It was too much to take in. The sense of hope that had filled me just a day before vanished, and I feared it would never return. The sound of the second plane hitting the tower will forever stay with me. It was so distinct, so horrifying. That sound changed the world. It changed everything.

And it changed me.

Following September 11th, the city and country rallied in outrage against the attackers. I had fond memories of people in San Francisco and New York City before then. Most were kind to me and accepted my inability to communicate, my immigrant-ness. After September 11th, people treated immigrants differently. Hatred seemed pervasive. People withdrew and showed less tolerance toward others. A lack of trust emerged—not just toward the group who had committed those atrocities, but toward all ethnicities.

CHAPTER 6

"I'M SORRY, BUT our fashion design program is full for the spring semester. You are welcome to come back again for the fall semester."

The woman at the FIT admissions office was helpful and patient, but at twenty-eight years of age, I had already waited three months for the city to recover from the 9/11 attacks, and I didn't have another six months to waste. The horror in New York City increased my determination and lowered my patience. It was now or never. I had to move forward.

"What else do you have that's related to fashion?" I asked.

"We have room in the textile design program. Is that something that would interest you?"

"Yes. I'll take it. What do I need to do?" I said without hesitation.

The admissions agent's eyebrows popped up. "Okay! Well, first, fill out this application and pay the deposit. Then submit your portfolio."

Crap! Portfolio?

"Um, can you give me a sample of what you are looking for?" My breathing quickened. I didn't want to appear naïve, but I wasn't sure what a portfolio even looked like. Maybe this obstacle was too big to overcome.

"I'll include the guidelines in your information packet," The admissions officer replied. Her warm and knowing smile suggested she'd read right through me. Obviously, I was not the first applicant to ask that question.

Signing up for the textile program marked a full circle moment.

It transported me back to my childhood, to the very essence of my undiscovered delight for textiles. Threads of passion, intuition, and determination wrapped me in the warmth of realization. I may have ventured into this realm with no formal art education, but I did have a background in textile and design. It had taken shape on that simple dirt floor amidst Grandma's tales and the soulful rhythm of her craft.

I had walked past an arts and crafts store called Pearl Paint on Canal Street near our apartment many times. But after leaving the FIT admissions office, I went inside. I was on a mission. Unsure of what I needed, I filled my basket with paper, colored pencils, fabric swatches, glue, and other supplies that might be helpful. Next, I stopped at the library to figure out what a textile design portfolio looked like.

Now I must go into the sacred place of art with zero experience.

Without a childhood education in the creative arts, I had never explored this side of myself. For the next three days, I locked myself away to create some kind of portfolio. With no prior experience, I had to rely on intuition. I made a few drawings and used the fabric to show how I would put color and texture together. With scraps of paper and fabric strewn everywhere, our tiny apartment looked like a tornado had blown through it. I could think of nothing else but getting into FIT, and my acceptance was based on turning these simple elements into a compelling portfolio.

Anxiety shot through my veins.

I can't let my fear stop me from moving forward.

Wei had encouraged me to show my authentic self. That evening, I held my breath and presented my work—my authentic self—to him.

"This is really good!" he exclaimed.

I sensed his sincerity, and his affirmation made my confidence soar. He became an encouraging art teacher in that moment. He was especially impressed with the collage I created by attaching a discarded computer keyboard I had picked up from a street corner to an abstract background. If it weren't for his support, I would never have believed I could become a designer.

Wei, my ponytailed lawyer, had attracted me for a reason. That reason was becoming clear, and so was my destiny.

✻

"I'm submitting my application and portfolio today."

Wei surely heard the anxiety in my voice. "That's great," he said, smiling. "I can go with you to drop it off. I don't mind being late to the office today."

"Thank you for giving me the courage to do this," I said. A strong sense of trepidation tempered my excitement. *What will they think of my portfolio and my background? Will I be enough? Will they even consider me?*

I didn't want to think about what other options I might have; this was all I wanted.

What seemed like months later, I had my answer. Spotting the FIT logo mixed in with our mail caused my hands to shake, making it almost impossible to open the envelope. When Wei returned from work that evening, I jumped into a frenzy, waving the FIT letter. "I got accepted! I can't believe it!"

Wei dropped his briefcase and joined my little celebration.

Once again, the thread of courage helped me overcome my latest obstacle. After quitting night school in Beijing, I could finally call Mother and tell her I was going to get a full college degree. The dream had finally come true for both of us.

✻

Wei suggested I create my own space to work on my college assignments. We browsed a few second-hand stores to find a basic desk small enough to fit in a corner of the apartment but large enough to accommodate my homework, drawings, and paintings.

The design program challenged me in new ways, unlocking a passion I never realized I had. It taught me what art is. It helped me understand that art allows self-expression in unique and authentic ways. Anyone can create art. The courses gave me confidence to express myself, and I came to understand that it is not about technique; it's about how I see things.

One assignment required creating a self-portrait. I love Matisse. His piece titled "The Dance" reminds me of me. It is so liberating, full of freedom and self-awareness. I followed Matisse's lead and created a self-portrait in a similar style. The project excited me. I felt alive in a whole new way.

I experienced a mind-blowing transformation during those years at FIT. The small corner of our apartment became one of my happy places as I explored and developed an unfamiliar part of myself.

The Home Fashion Products Association had a close partnership with FIT, offering annual scholarships to students. In my senior year, I finally decided to apply. The scholarship application process included an interview with a panel of ten board members. Applicants presented their portfolios and answered questions. During my time at FIT, my portfolio and my English had improved, but I still felt nervous and scared to speak.

"What do you want to do with your career?" asked the CEO of a fourth-generation family-owned textile manufacturing company.

"I want to learn as much as possible and one day have my own business like you," I told him.

The panelists smiled at my bold statement and nodded. I even got a chuckle out of the CEO.

Running businesses in China gave me confidence, but the FIT program revealed my passion for design, fashion, and textiles. I believe my passion shone through that day, and that's why I received a $1,500 scholarship. The boost of confidence that came along with it was the real value, the spark that propelled me forward. I walked home that afternoon knowing I could do well.

I set a goal to learn everything I could at FIT and graduate early. I wanted the same kind of real-world experience that taught me about business in China. Hands-on learning better suited my impatient, active mind. I took the maximum number of credits each semester and attended year-round, which allowed me to attain my four-year degree in just three years.

"I am so proud of you, Jing-Jing." The emotion in Mother's voice was palpable, touching my heart across thousands of miles through the phone. My parents were never comfortable praising me. The culture of their generation made it hard for them to give positive feedback, causing my generation to feel like we were never good enough. Being a striver and perfectionist works well in business, but not so much in life.

"To graduate summa cum laude is just . . . is just wonderful," she said. She understood the hard work that title represented. We both knew I had finally found my place in the world. It made her proud to tell her friends how well I'd done, giving her the chance to brag about me. When I moved them to Beijing, things changed a bit in our relationship. Their pride in me grew. Although that was important to them, they still found it hard to express themselves.

During my last semester, I entered several design competitions hosted by FIT and sponsored by industry-leading companies. Every award included a small sum of money, but the real benefit came through the recognition it brought and the opportunity to interact with these companies professionally. I won the first competition I entered with Sunbrella and received the first-place award for my textile design. The experience gave me an inside look at the industry.

"We'd like you to come to our showroom next week," The Sunbrella production manager told me during a phone call, making my whole body tingle. "We produced a selection of swatches for your review."

Sitting in that showroom, seeing and touching my designs on those swatches, seemed surreal. I finally belonged. I started with no design background, and there I was, transformed. I was now a player talking to the big players, and they were taking me seriously.

I won another award for a carpet design and received an honorable mention at a big textile industry show. Seeing my designs come to life provided further confirmation that I had discovered my destiny. All the threads I'd gathered and woven together were forming a beautiful life tapestry. I felt fulfilled.

✳

The Textile Building at 295 Fifth Avenue became a special place for me. Known as the "Holy Grail" for textile students with big dreams, it housed the offices and showrooms of seventy-eight prestigious textile companies. I printed out a stack of resumes and hung out in the lobby when I wasn't in class. I still remember how anxious I was trying to talk to people passing through the lobby, but I didn't let that stop me from approaching them.

"Hi, I'm Jing-Jing. I'll be graduating soon from FIT as a textile designer. Please take a resume."

I worked hard to find a job at a company that would sponsor my work visa. I had a new dream: to open my own company's showroom in that building someday. But the uncertainty I felt about my future in a foreign country and my frustration at not getting any responses clouded my vision. My previous jobs had come easily, so this uphill battle presented a new challenge.

How do I overcome the obstacle of not having the right visa?

The answer was to keep trying, to do my best, no matter what. The shrill sound of our telephone had come to signify a mix of hope and anxiety about this, and I jumped to answer every time it rang. And finally, one call proved that my hard work had paid off.

"Hi, I'm calling for Gu . . . Guo . . . " The man on the other end was clearly American and had trouble with my formal Chinese first name, Guojing (pronounced Goo-ah-jing). I changed it to Jenny after graduating from FIT because no one could pronounce it. I really didn't think about how that decision would impact my identity. I just wanted to make it easier for others and for myself. Later, I realized that it is not really the name that matters; it is about how you feel about yourself. I love the Jenny part of my life, and I love the Jing part. Both have been important to my journey.

Unfortunately, even my short last name proved challenging.

"Hi," I replied to my caller. "You can call me Jenny. And my last name is Zhu, like Jewel."

"Oh, that makes it easy. Well, I'd like you to come in for an interview."

"Great!" I hesitated for a moment, and then asked him the question I dreaded. "I am a Chinese citizen. Is your company willing to sponsor a work visa for me?" Better to get this question answered right up front. I held my breath.

"We've had other workers on visas. Shouldn't be an issue."

We set a time for an interview and hung up. I immediately launched into a celebration of joy-filled dancing and laughter. Finally! I didn't even care what the job was; I just wanted the job! A few days later, I met with the man who had called me. Mr. Hoffman was the CEO of a family-owned business that he had started with his brother. His great-grandparents had been immigrants too. His accent, a mix of his Brooklyn upbringing and his Jewish heritage, made me wonder if he too had his own style of Jinglish-like made-up words.

He explained that my fluency in Chinese would be beneficial to his dealings with their suppliers in China. He wanted me to start right away. He offered me an entry-level job on the spot, but I had to finish my finals before I could begin. Thankfully, my professors were very supportive, which allowed me to start just a few weeks later.

❖

The real world of the textile industry turned out to be far more complex than the classroom assignments or the fabrics woven on my grandma's loom. Like a sponge, I was eager to learn how to transform designs into beautiful bedding and how the business worked. Grateful for the opportunity, I was determined to show that Mr. Hoffman's decision to hire me was the right one. I had to prove myself. The effort I poured into my studies rolled seamlessly into my new job. My eagerness to learn and my strong work ethic were not lost on the family I now worked for.

"Are you still here?" Mr. Hoffman stopped by my desk on his way out one evening. "Heck, I might hand the company over to you someday!" He chuckled at his joke.

In my typical 110 percent way, I took ownership of my job. I didn't watch the clock like the others did to see if it was time to leave. No matter what, I would do my best.

"Jenny, I've heard a lot of positive comments about how hard you work. I'm impressed by how much you've improved since you joined us." Mr. Hoffman didn't give praise often, so his appreciation of my effort made me happy. "You've been with us for almost a year. I'd like to promote you to the manager of our key accounts."

In my new job, I maintained the company's relationships with big accounts like Walmart and Target. By my second year, I earned more than double my original salary—the most I'd made since coming to the US. It changed our lives, and it felt good.

Not long after stepping into my new role, the early morning light became a regular part of my routine. Before the city stirred to life, I was already deep in communication with overseas factories. This responsibility became a hands-on learning experience for me, exposing me to the intricacies of the business world.

The significance of turning a vision into a tangible product became one of the most profound lessons I absorbed. My career wasn't just about creating; it was about understanding the entire process from ideation to the final touch. I had to ensure designs weren't merely beautiful on paper—they had to be feasible for manufacturing and appealing to the market. The dance between creativity and production proved delicate. While a design's innovation held paramount importance, its transition from paper to reality required collaboration with factories and an understanding of their capacities and limitations.

Negotiation involved more than a transactional interaction; it became an art form. I learned that everything is possible through negotiation. Beyond prices and deadlines, it meant cultivating lasting relationships and mutual respect. Building trust with manufacturers meant understanding their needs and challenges and ensuring they felt valued in our partnership. It was a two-way street, with both parties seeking a balance that provided stability and met market demands.

As I reached my thirty-third birthday, I felt like I wanted to be a mom. The clock was ticking. If I wanted to have a child, I'd have to do it before I turned thirty-five. I knew we would never be ready. I don't think anyone is ever truly ready to bring a child into the world. But the timing looked good. We were financially stable, I had always wanted to have a child, and my experience with baby Olivia strengthened that desire.

Our son was born in 2007, presenting me with the thread of motherhood. Complications with my pregnancy and the eventual birth of my son by cesarean section required I take time to heal. During my maternity leave, I had time to think about my life. The idea of entrepreneurship had been in my head since I read that magazine article as a teen. And Vera Wang's story pushed my ambition into overdrive. But now, with a new baby, I had a lot more to consider. Why would I leave a steady job that paid a six-figure salary? But if I kept working, who would look after my son? I had to resolve the internal struggle by figuring out how to weave motherhood and entrepreneurship together without unravelling.

I didn't like the status quo. I wanted the challenge of something new, to explore uncharted territory. At the time, I wasn't fully aware of my desire to explore, but I was always thinking about what came next. Starting a business seemed like the next logical step toward financial freedom. But my fears were very real. I wanted to protect my son and our future. I believed it would mean stability for me in this foreign land and control over my future. It would mean fulfilling the dream that was born in that cotton field in China.

"If I don't start a business now while our son is young, I will never get around to doing it. We will never be 100 percent prepared," I reasoned more to myself than to Wei one evening. I wasn't sure he was even listening. He seemed more distracted of late.

The baby changed me, igniting my motherly instinct and giving me a new lens for my view of life. His birth changed Wei too. He started talking more about going back to China. But I wanted my son to live here with me, and I wanted to start my business here. After getting my first job with Mr. Hoffman, I became confident I could get another job if a business didn't work out. I felt I had a chance to make my dream of being in fashion come true. I was finally thriving like I had in Beijing, and I wanted a chance to prove myself here. Wei thought China would be better for his career. We had two different goals. We began arguing more about what we each thought was better.

We each had a choice to make.

I needed to jump in and see what I was made of, ignoring any fear. I decided to jump in, just as I had with our marriage. I knew if I didn't make the leap, the thought of *what if* would haunt me for the rest of my life. That would be much worse than trying it and failing.

I knew I would learn from the experience, no matter how it turned out.

CHAPTER 7

"**I**'**M THINKING ABOUT** starting my own company." Just a few weeks after I returned to work from maternity leave in early 2008, I made a passing comment to my coworker, Thomas.

"Really? I owned a textile company once." Thomas suggested we discuss the details at lunch. He seemed to know a lot about starting a business in the US, and he was very eager to help. "I have a relationship with buyers. I can help you manage the business, do sales, find a warehouse, and handle the paperwork to set up the company."

Through previous dealings in my job, I had established a relationship with a manufacturer in China. *We could make this work*, I mused.

"I don't have any money to invest," he told me, "but I'll help you get it started for an eight percent stake in the company."

Okay. I have a manufacturer and help with a sales team. I'm ready!

Bursting with naivete and eagerness to get started, I agreed. I trusted Thomas would help me, and the partnership looked great. Even though I didn't know Thomas well, he had helped on a project for one of my big customers. A soft-spoken father of two young children with a stay-at-home wife, it was easy to trust him. Like me, he was an immigrant, so we had a connection.

Thomas wanted to be CEO and make me the president. I didn't care about titles; I just wanted to start my company and put my designs into the world. We jumped in with only an operating agreement and a handshake. I relied entirely on his experience as an immigrant who had started a business before, and that gave me confidence that he would take us in the right direction.

Throughout my journey, I learned that sometimes naivete is powerful. From my first job carrying bricks to applying to the Fashion Institute of Technology with no portfolio, I discovered that not knowing what I'm getting myself into makes me unafraid to do it. And deep inside, I believe if I don't at least try, nothing will happen.

Starting my company seemed no different from any of my past endeavors. Even as a new mom with a young baby, I would give it my all.

If it works, it will be rewarding. If not, I will gain wisdom and receive another gift of learning.

Sometimes we overthink the risks, and then we don't move. I never wanted to regret what I didn't do. I still toyed with the idea of designing wedding dresses, but the reality of becoming a designer was a stretch. The idea stuck in my head, much the way most women have a dream about their wedding dress. I liked to think outside of the box. If I couldn't be in fashion, then I wanted to design something for home textiles that would reflect the same fashion sense.

Thomas had a background in bedding, and I had four years of work experience in home textile design. I planned to design bedding products here in the US and manufacture them in China through our partner, Dan.

The next few weeks flew by. We found a 4,000-square-foot space in New Jersey, and I wired the funds to rent it. Thomas handled all the paperwork to start the business, and I let him. I didn't like doing paperwork, so I didn't pay close attention to what he was doing.

I didn't know what I didn't know.

Like any startup company, our first year met with both triumph and defeat. I handled logistics, and Thomas handled sales. I hoped big box stores would feature our products on their shelves, but at the time, a recession gripped the economy. It gave me a serious reality check. Low consumer demand clogged store inventories, and no one would give us a chance as a new vendor.

My designs were unique because of my bold, experimental themes, making them a tough fit for the traditional customer base of the big box stores. I had zero data on whether the products would be successful, but I wanted to develop a fantasy, fanciful, and frilly style. The decision came from a design perspective, not a business perspective.

Although motherhood had been delightful in the beginning, it got harder after I started the business. I constantly battled with guilt. My son was still a baby. I worked too much and traveled too much. As a person who puts 100 percent into everything I do, the inability to be 100 percent in my business and 100 percent with my son was torture. I felt like the worst mom in the world. If I could have spoken with other entrepreneur moms, I would have understood that we all go through those feelings.

I took annual weeks-long trips to China during the first seven years to work with our suppliers. I found it really difficult to leave my son for that long. The trips were demanding too. One trip during the height of summer involved going into factory storage areas in 100-degree heat. I think I lost about fifteen pounds. I was so busy that I didn't eat or drink much. At one point, I felt faint and struggled to walk, so I sat on the floor in a hallway. The manager put me in his car and took me to a nearby hospital. I ended up being admitted with a 104-degree fever and severe dehydration. I recovered, but it was a crazy experience.

Back in New York, Thomas found me checking inventory in the warehouse late one afternoon.

"I think we can make this company bigger," he said, holding my gaze.

I could tell he was trying to read my reaction. I agreed with him, but something felt a little off. Back in Beijing, I had learned to listen to my intuition, but that time, I didn't. I was focused on finishing my work so I could head home for the evening.

Later that evening, once my son fell asleep, I flopped onto the couch next to Wei.

"I want to return to China soon," he announced. "I want to go back to pursue opening my own law firm."

We had been married for ten years but had grown apart over the past twelve months. I sensed an increased restlessness in him. He had often talked about going back to China, and at times I felt he was too idealistic. His announcement didn't come as a surprise. It was lousy timing though. Shifting to his own law firm would require starting over for him—just as I finally began to feel at home in the US. I didn't want to go back. It would mean starting all over again in China for me too.

Years of being together allow you to learn more about a person and about yourself. When we came to San Francisco, we had a shared vision for a better life. Since arriving, and working through identity issues, I had finally started coming back to *me*, discovering who I really was, and deciding what my next steps should be. Wei was always looking for his next steps too. The dynamic shifted as I found my stride.

Wei always encouraged me, but neither one of us had anticipated the kind of transformation I underwent. For the first time in my life, I'd found an intersection between passion and work. Maternal instincts drove how I thought about my future and my son's future. I felt I needed to control my own life as an entrepreneur and as a mother, and that was challenging. Wei's parents and mine planned to come from China to help care for our son, alternating six months at a time. If we divorced and Wei moved back to China, his parents would no longer be eligible for a visa, so they wouldn't be able to help.

It gave me a lot to think about.

I firmly believed that our son's future lay here with me in the US, where he could have access to education and opportunities that would shape his life in a positive way. Wei shared this belief. He had a profound love for our son and cherished the role of being a father. In the midst of our personal and emotional challenges, we found common ground in an unwavering commitment to our son's well-being. We agreed that he should stay with me in the US, where he could thrive and grow.

Wei accepted that decision, even though, as an attorney, he had the legal means to pursue a different path.

My mind drifted through the obstacles that lay ahead. Wondering how I would walk this path alone, my grandma's feet came to mind. In ancient Chinese tradition, it was customary to break and tightly bind the feet of young girls to alter their shape and size. Grandma had endured that process. What struck me most was how her small, triangle-shaped lotus feet, which had endured the painful and drawn-out process of foot binding, carried her through her day and powered the antique weaving loom. It seemed to have no impact on her ability to weave fabric, stories, and her life. She had overcome a crushing obstacle. Could I overcome mine?

❉

Not long after our company passed its first anniversary, Thomas began acting strange. His right heel sprang into nervous, rapid tapping whenever he sat. He often raked his right hand through his thick black hair, pulling the skin of his receding hairline taut across his skull. I noticed, but I was so overwhelmed with work that I didn't think to ask if he was okay.

One afternoon, he came into my office and stood in front of my desk. His eyes darted around the room, never meeting mine for more than a second or two.

"I want twenty-two percent of the company." He swiped at a bead of sweat rolling down his temple, absorbing it with the frayed cuff of his dress shirt. I'd set the heat low even though it was winter, keeping my office cool, saving every penny I could.

Why is he sweating?

"Well, okay, Thomas. But I don't think it's the right time." It seemed like a strange request. He knew full well that we had been in business for just over a year. We had experienced the typical startup trials, but we were slowly growing. "If you want twenty-two percent, you will have to buy into it." I knew how much he was taking home from the business, so I knew he still had no money to invest.

"I'm so grateful for this opportunity you've given me, Jenny. My wife and family are so grateful," he said.

I smiled and nodded, hoping to hide the puzzled look on my face as he turned to leave. The leftover dim sum I'd brought from home had gone cold hours before, giving me little comfort as I tried to untangle the odd conversation we had just had. Pulling my cardigan tight around my waist did nothing to ease the strange feeling that lingered in my gut.

Back to work. We've got orders to fill to meet our deadlines.

Early one morning about a week later, Thomas strode into my office and sat in a chair across from me. He wore a dark-colored suit with a fresh white button-down shirt, the collar secured by a red and gray striped necktie. He always wore a suit, but today his look was crisper and polished, giving him a serious air.

"Good morning. What's up?" Curiosity pulled me forward in my chair, and my eyes fixed on his face.

He pulled a folded letter from the inside breast pocket of his jacket. Again, he wouldn't look me in the eye. As he struggled to steady his nervous hands, he read the letter.

He culminated with, "You are terminated, effective immediately."

"What? You're kidding, right?" I thought it was some kind of April Fool's joke. It just didn't make sense. "Thomas, what is going on here?"

He recited a list of the reasons for firing me. He read them quickly, but the words that rang in my ears were *fraudulent activities* and *I am the rightful majority owner.* "You will be deported because of your visa. Please pack your things and leave, or I'll call the police to remove you," he concluded.

"What are you talking about? What . . .?" I couldn't breathe.

Thomas gave me no time to digest what was happening. Within moments, two police officers walked in and stood on either side of him. They must have been waiting for his call.

"I'm sorry, ma'am, but you have to leave the premises," the first officer said.

"Leave the keys to the company car on the desk," Thomas commanded.

"But he is a minority owner. I am the majority owner. This is my company!" A frenetic shrill laced my words. Desperation seeped through my pores as I began to drown in the unannounced tsunami of potential legal action.

"Do you have any documentation to prove that?" the second officer asked.

"Not with me."

"I suggest you hire an attorney, ma'am. Now please, come with me."

White-hot anger seared my brain. I felt nauseous. After a year and a half of crazy hard work, long hours away from my son, and my heart and soul poured into the business, I was being kicked out. I could not even get home because Thomas seized my car.

I moved away from my desk like a zombie.

My team watched in horror as two police officers escorted me through the office. Their fear hung in the air like a dense fog. I could only imagine what was going through their minds, but I couldn't reassure them.

In need of a ride, I put my box of personal items down on the sidewalk and called Rachel, the second immigrant I had hired. She and a couple of other employees met me in the parking lot. Someone volunteered to drive me home.

I gave Rachel a hug. "Don't worry about your visa. I'll make sure it's taken care of." I did my best to fight back tears.

I don't remember much about how I got home. When we pulled up to the curb, I stepped onto the sidewalk in front of my apartment and dragged my box of belongings from the back seat. Fury raged through my body, causing me to shake. I was unsure whether my knees would hold me upright much longer. I managed to hold it together until my team member's car turned the corner and slipped out of sight. I fell to my knees. The scream that exploded from deep in my lungs frightened the finches perching in the row of now barren azalea bushes lining the walkway.

It frightened me too.

I'm not sure how I shook off the shock. On my journey from a small Chinese village to Beijing, to San Francisco, and now to New York City, I'd experienced nothing as personal and devastating as this.

My black patterned tights had become stuck to the frozen concrete where my knees had landed. I peeled them away and struggled back to my feet. I needed to walk. I needed to breathe. As my mind cleared, I assessed my situation. Thank God Wei was still here, and his parents were staying with us, not mine. Mother would have read my face and insisted on knowing what was wrong. I would have had nothing to tell her. I had no idea what was wrong!

Literally overnight, naivete became the biggest obstacle I had ever faced in my life. And I wasn't sure I could overcome this one.

CHAPTER 8

WEI RUSHED HOME after my frantic call to his office. "Tell me exactly what he said to you." He remained calm and focused, sitting at our kitchen table while I paced the floor. With pen in hand, he questioned me and captured all the details I could remember. "Did you get a copy of the letter?"

"No! It happened so fast. I didn't even think . . ."

"What could he possibly mean by fraudulent activity?"

"I don't know. Let me think." As my mind churned, details started coming back to me. "He said they will deport me. He said he reported me to the FBI and Homeland Security, that they are watching me now." It's the fear of every immigrant to be sent back like a criminal with nothing.

"It's okay, Jing. I'll look into that when I get back to the office." Wei did his best to reassure both of us.

"The only thing I can think of is that I signed a document that needed his signature. I signed his name. He was rushing out of the office. We needed to get it signed and submitted. It was for one of our employees. Her work visa . . ." My mind raced.

"Did he know you did that?"

"Yes. We agreed to apply for the visa. He was rushing to a meeting, and he said I should sign his signature. I didn't think it was a big deal."

Is that what this is about?

Talking through the situation helped unlock my mind. As my ability to think returned, survival instinct kicked in. After Wei headed back to his office, I called several attorneys.

"We need to file an emergency injunction to stop any further action on his part," one attorney told me. She had a tough-minded, no-bullshit style, experience in business law and agreed to take my case. It would be very expensive, but it was my only option if I wanted my company back.

Sitting in her office the next morning, my hands trembled as I wrote one of the largest personal checks I'd ever signed. Wei and I were savers, having both come from meager upbringings. We were proud of the savings and investments we'd made on our way to reaching our financial goals. Neither of us had envisioned spending our hard-earned money on something like this.

Disbelief consumed me. My blind trust and naivete merged into a dagger that wedged in my stomach. I'd always had an overactive imagination, but this was far beyond anything I could fathom. Victim mentality pushed its way into my head. And for now, I had little choice but to let it in.

In the days that followed, I received a call from one of Thomas's former employees. He told me Thomas owed him significant back pay, and that Thomas's business career was marked by deals that placed him in deep debt. This employee claimed that a court martial enforced repayment of that debt, so Thomas was desperate.

I wanted Thomas in jail. Nothing else would soothe my fury.

Thomas and I fought for three months, enduring angry phone conversations and heated negotiations through our attorneys. He stirred turmoil among my employees and customers. He said I forged his signature with Homeland Security for the visa application. I couldn't stop wondering if he had set me up, knowing that signature would get me in trouble. He made it sound as though I did this behind his back. I struggled with a deep feeling of betrayal.

I had an eighteen-month-old son, a dissolving marriage, and now I was about to lose my business. In those three months, I didn't eat or sleep. Weight dropped from my already lean body. During that time,

I don't think I fully exhaled. Nothing comforted me. Most of those months unfolded in a blur. I just remember going to court. For the first time in my life, I was in a court building, sitting on a bench outside a courtroom, waiting to face a judge.

Is this real? Is it really happening?

The only corporate document in my possession was an operating agreement that named me, Thomas, and our third partner, Dan, the manufacturer in China. Thomas had set up the company without clearly identifying me as the majority owner on any of the documents. It left him sitting pretty as part owner.

"You have to decide how you want to proceed." My attorney leaned in close and lowered her voice. "You can buy him out or go to trial, which could take years and a lot of money. Chances are you'd end up with the same result." The dagger in my stomach twisted at the thought of giving this person my money, but I wanted it to be over.

The final settlement resulted in my buying him out and cutting him off completely from any further connection to me or my company. When the judge voted in my favor, I thought I would feel relief and maybe a little happiness. Instead, a sense of emptiness seeped into the void left by anger and frustration. Fear had taken its toll, and the experience shook me to my very core. Trust would not come easily for quite a while—self-trust in particular. I began questioning everything I thought I believed.

Lying in bed, eyes wide open at two in the morning, staring at the ceiling, I questioned myself too. The threads I had so carefully woven were being stretched to their limits, fraying from the pressure. I wasn't sure they were strong enough. I wasn't sure I was strong enough.

✢

Since the first morning I woke up in San Francisco, I had sensed a kindred connection to other immigrants. Our journeys started in different places but somehow took similar paths converging on American soil. The melting pot culture didn't always mean we melted together perfectly, but we understood each other. That belief made it difficult for me to understand how one immigrant could do such horrible things to another. Try as I might, I struggled to reconcile it. Thomas faced enormous trouble, but that didn't give him a license to abuse me or anyone. Hatred had its hooks in me for quite a while. Anger filled me to the brim, bubbling over onto those around me. I was defeated, drained, and out of money with a baby to care for. Sometimes I wondered if it was all worth it. The unexpected blow beat me down.

Maybe this time I just accept defeat?

I thought about taking my baby and leaving. I drifted through those dark days at rock bottom with no sense of direction. I am not sure what got me through it. Wei and I were separating, and he was moving back to China, but instead of leaving right away, he stayed to help me through the lawsuit. His support lit a bright spot in the darkness, and I was so appreciative. I lost a husband through our divorce, but I gained a good friend. Our relationship continues to this day as a sincere and supportive collaboration.

As the dust settled and my desire to succeed peeked out from under the rubble, I climbed back into the driver's seat of my life. I refused to accept defeat. I chose to view my rock-bottom experience as a solid foundation on which to grow. If I wanted to be a successful entrepreneur, many more challenges would lay ahead. With the worst behind me, it was easier to see all I had learned from the experience. It seemed odd, but I almost wanted to thank Thomas for teaching me how to survive as a leader, a mom, an ex-wife—everything. Rock bottom ended up giving me such confidence. The tapestry I'd worked so hard to weave had not only withstood the storm, it gave me a soft place to land and recover. Every one of those threads contributed to my resilience.

Sometimes the only path to deep growth is through the darkness.

CHAPTER 9

WHAT WILL *they think of me? Will they still trust me? Will they stay?* I had so much to recover from. I wondered how I would give myself and my team the confidence to keep going, to get out of this mess.

If I give up, I will regret this for the rest of my life.

I had serious popcorn brain during my drive to work on the first morning after the settlement. Months of drama, lawyers, and lies had taken a toll on my customers and my employees. The knot in my stomach tightened as I pulled into the parking lot. The nervous energy flowing through my body surprised me. My trembling hands dropped my keys twice before I even got out of the car.

Thank God I didn't spill my coffee.

I was a hot mess inside but didn't want it to show. It was the last thing my staff needed from me. Three months on an emotional rollercoaster had taken a significant toll not just on me but also on my team.

"Welcome back, Jenny!" Sheela, the talented designer I had hired straight out of college, greeted me with a voice filled with relief as I walked through the front door. She embraced me as others lined up behind her to do the same.

Their hugs were more than a simple greeting; they were an intense and heartfelt expression of their own stress, a silent plea for stability amidst the chaos. Their hugs, so imploring, gave me a tangible sense of their loyalty. That feeling became deeply etched into my soul.

This. This is why I decided to keep moving forward, no matter what.

My office was a mess; papers and files were strewn in desperate piles on every open surface, a parting gift from my former partner.

Rachel snatched up a half-filled garbage bag from the corner. "I'm sorry, Jenny. I started cleaning it up but . . ."

"No worries. It's not your mess." I hoped my smile would give her some comfort. "I'll take care of it." Cleaning up that physical chaos was therapy for the emotional chaos that had consumed me. Nervous energy and overwhelm left my body as I cleaned. It became an act of leadership, of regaining control. Sitting once again at my no tidy desk, a sigh escaped my mouth with an awkward flapping noise. I laughed. I couldn't remember the last time I laughed. It felt good.

The list of to-dos threatened to overwhelm me, but I couldn't let them. Now that I had regained control, I needed to prioritize, delegate, and start rebuilding. With a small customer base, it was critical to rebuild those relationships first. I addressed the issue directly in a letter to them, stating that whatever they may have heard was not true. I called each customer and addressed their concerns. I hired a new EVP of sales and empowered him to speak directly about the lawsuit whenever it came up. No putting our heads in the sand. I had nothing to hide and everything to gain by being transparent.

I think I was born with a healthy amount of determination, but the fire of my experience forged something stronger, a steely fortitude. I gained an advantage by facing down the biggest challenge of my life. I wasn't exactly bulletproof, but I was getting pretty damn close.

❊

Decision-making wasn't over. I still had my second partner, Dan, who owned the manufacturing facility in China. Because of our exclusive partnership contract, I didn't have the freedom to source from other suppliers. Dan's prices were very high because he wanted more margin at his factory level. The pricing made it difficult to be competitive and get my products placed during a crippling recession. His pricing also prevented me from making a positive margin, so we owed Dan money from past orders. The more we sold, the more we owed him. When I added that debt to the amount I spent on legal fees, I began to wonder if my company would make it.

Dan's goals focused on making money and building his factory. Mine focused on offering affordable, good-quality products and figuring out how to restore my business. Our different goals forced me to make another tough decision. My attorney once again explained my options; I could bankrupt the company and let it go or buy Dan out. A friend suggested I file for bankruptcy, walk away from everything, wipe the slate clean, and find a job.

But the situation was not that simple. When I had worked with my two female partners in China, I learned the importance of true partnership. We stood by each other and knew the value of loyalty. Even though my experience with Thomas left me reeling, I wanted to improve my remaining partnerships. Thomas had tried to talk Dan into joining him to take over the company and keep me out, but Dan refused. He didn't trust Thomas. Dan stood by me, and that meant a lot. We would both lose if I shut Dan down.

It was not fair to Dan to walk away from the sizable sum we owed him. Also, I couldn't let my employees down. Shutting down the business would have a devastating impact on them. It would mean walking away from the dream I'd been weaving my entire life.

I had to try every possible resolution.

As always, I believed the only solution was to keep moving forward, to do my best, no matter what. Dan told me he wanted to get out of our contract. I offered to buy him out on a payment plan. It created a lot of pressure because all that debt would fall on me alone. Under our new agreement, I could source from other suppliers, and he had to be more competitive. This creative solution helped my company improve our margin and pay our debt. It helped everyone involved. Although it was a crazy time, I didn't think about the hardships. I just did what I had to do to survive.

Carrying the weight of my life in those days was the hardest work I've ever done. My mind drifted back to Beijing, to my boyfriend and the dry cleaning business. Survival looked so different back then. Betrayal, however, cut just as deeply.

✳

The phrase, "Um, how do you say . . ." has always frustrated me for two reasons. I hated not knowing the right word. I still do. And I hated being slowed down. My mind raced ahead, but the English words didn't come quickly enough. When I returned to my company, I needed to interact with customers and give presentations to management groups at large companies. The language barrier often reared its ugly head as I struggled to express what I really meant. My nervousness caused plenty of *oops* moments, making me feel foolish. With so much on the line, I worried about how I would deliver presentations to important customers to win their business.

During one meeting with a big customer, I decided to see if I could turn the language barrier to my advantage. I shifted my focus from language to showing my passion through my trademark Jinglish—my gut-level approach to powerful communication As I stood in front of a room of management executives, I hoped they would see and feel beyond the words I spoke. Like so many of our customers, they were focused on price, but I wanted to drive home how we added value through our affordable quality products and service.

"I don't like to lower our level of quality. There is so much shitty quality in the marketplace already." Yikes! I was on a roll, and the curse word just slipped out. My face flushed as my eyes darted around the room.

Most people smiled and nodded in agreement. I'd made my point.

One company executive approached me after the meeting. "Jenny, you and your company are a diamond in the rough." He shook my hand and thanked me for my candid remarks.

It worked. My passion for our work—even with the curse word— overcame the language barrier. The risk paid off. They saw and felt my drive and my pride in our small but mighty team. They saw and sensed my promise of reliable delivery and my drive to exceed expectations. When I told them we do what we say and go the extra mile, they felt my conviction. I had transformed Jinglish from an obstacle into an advantage. All the other threads I'd woven into my life made sense; they served a clear purpose. Never in my life had I thought that my Jinglish would become such an important thread, adding strength and purpose to my life and my business. My grandma's chuckle of delight echoed in my mind.

✳

Within a year of my return, I realized our business model was becoming a challenge. We had a regional footprint focused on brick-and-mortar stores for sales and distribution through retailers like QVC, Home Goods, and Macy's. If the purchasing team liked a design we presented to them, they would place a bulk order. However, the recession that began in 2008 created a huge backlog of market inventory. The big brands already had an established supplier base, and many were trying to shrink their supplier base rather than find new ones like us.

Existing customers continued to focus solely on price. I fought to stand my ground, continuing to offer good quality products at affordable prices. Lowering our quality or price was simply not an option in my mind. Sourcing globally improved our margin significantly, but it still wasn't enough. This stance limited our ability to grow, so I started exploring other business models and options.

The recession persisted, pushing the direct-to-consumer bubble toward its bursting point. We didn't have the funds to build a direct-to-consumer website and business model anyway. It seemed we had hit a wall. If we couldn't go the direct-to-consumer route, then we'd have to consider placement on big box store websites. The e-commerce model was a risky shift for the textile industry, and very few of our competitors wanted to jump in. However, my thread of risk-taking was tested and true, so I viewed it differently. I believed the obstacles hid a significant opportunity.

I wanted to break through the wall, convinced the opportunities on the other side would be worth the risk. But the risk was particularly enormous for my small business.

A sense of loneliness filled my head and heart under the weight of this critical decision. Not only did I face life alone as a single mother, but I had no one to discuss business with. Thoughts of how to make the business survive and take care of my baby consumed me. They were the only two things on my mind. I had no choice, which I believe made me stronger. I kept reminding myself to look forward, not back.

I had to get my son settled into preschool while restoring trust in my customers and my team. Pressure ran high, but I always felt I could do it. Personal loneliness sat heavily on my shoulders, but I would not lower the bar just to "find him a dad." I wanted to find a man who was good for both of us. As parents, we tend to live for our kids. We must live for ourselves too. I refused to be co-dependent out of desperation. The way I see it, you must make yourself happy first, which then gives you the choice of whether to partner.

Life as a single mom was a guilt-ridden season. I felt like I missed so much of my son's childhood. I learned that guilt doesn't help the situation. Children need to see a good example of how you live, your work ethic, and how you treat others. There's more to it than just being at home with the baby. It's about the quality of your relationship and what you model for them. Part of my guilt came from wishing I had more patience with my son. Most times, I was just drained. I wanted to make myself successful to show him how he could be successful too. But I came to understand that no matter whether I worked, had a fancy title, or owned a company, I would teach him every day through my behavior. That is what affects children the most.

Business decisions grew more complex, and the stakes were high. Long days pushed me further into isolation. Sitting at my desk in the early evenings, I sometimes wondered what Mother prepared for my son at dinner or if he played at the park that day. My mind drifted back to the fields in my village, and a vision emerged of my mother working so hard, teaching full-time, and tending the crops by moonlight. Her days were long too. The similarities in our life journeys surprised me. Had she felt guilty and alone too?

✳

Money was tight, so I always paid our debt and the team first. Traveling for meetings meant I had to be extremely frugal. I searched long and hard for the cheapest hotels and flights with no regard for convenience. The cheapest flights were always after midnight.

On of my trips to meet with a big customer, the clock on the dash of my rental car glowed a green 2:05 a.m. when I rolled into the parking lot of a cheap hotel. My arrival attracted the attention of the rather rough-looking crowd hanging around the main entrance. *Why were these people out here at this hour?* My heart raced as I gingerly maneuvered my slender Asian body and travel bag through the crowd, being extra careful not to bump into anyone. I instinctively held my breath to avoid inhaling whatever they were smoking.

After an awkward sprint down the hallway in stilettos, I squeezed myself and my bag into the room and slammed the door behind me, turning to latch every lock into place. I dropped my bag on the bed, where it instantly tumbled into the center of the bowl-shaped mattress. I moved every piece of furniture that wasn't bolted down in front of the door, all the while praying that a fire wouldn't break out. Only then did I stop to catch my breath. What a headline that would be: Asian business owner dies in fire at a seedy hotel.

Nice.

Even with my best efforts to secure my safety, I didn't sleep the rest of the night. Lying in that bed listening to the banging and arguments all around me, I made a promise to myself: I would never do this again. No matter what, I would put my safety first. I flew home the next evening feeling like a threadbare dishrag. I eased into the driver's seat of my car, fighting to keep my eyes open. On the highway, I changed lanes and sideswiped a truck. The collision sheared my outside mirror clean off. We both pulled over to exchange information. If the truck driver hadn't stopped, I would have sat on the side of the highway and cried.

Those were some tough times. I often wanted to cry. My lack of business advisers and resources put me at a disadvantage during a critical time in my young company's history. We were short on financial resources. Survival necessitated making margins to reinvest in the business. And I had no one to learn from or trust. Once again, obstacles piled up. I was running out of options, but I knew I had to take action to survive.

✳

The e-commerce and omni-channel model had downsides: we had to maintain the inventory and drop ship one order at a time directly to the customer's home. We had no idea how much each product would sell, so we had to maintain inventory of every product. But the upsides were significant: my design and products would be on big-box store websites with unlimited shelf space, and the sites attracted a broader audience with more diverse tastes in design. I was always proud of our designs. I remember thinking, *This is the way we will control our own destiny.* It was our chance to build and serve the e-commerce marketplace.

We took that chance and reached out to the team at Kohls.com. We presented them with some unique products. To our delight, they were excited. They saw an opportunity in our design and quality.

Everybody I spoke with in the industry thought the e-commerce model was impossible. I seemed to connect with every naysayer on the planet.

"How the hell are you going to ship one piece at a time? That will be extremely expensive!"

"You'll erode your margin without meeting factory order minimums."

"How will you build that infrastructure? Manage inventory?"

"What if your product doesn't sell? You'll be screwed."

They were right; we were taking a significant risk. The success rate was crazy low. But I thought if we could figure out how to do it, then we would be in great shape. The e-commerce business model forced a huge mental shift for the industry, and most of our competitors walked away. I embraced the challenge, wanting to figure out how to get it done. And figuring it out early in the game made all the difference. It became a new adventure. If I hadn't taken that risk, my company would not be here today. My risk-taking thread became even stronger through the experience.

We were finally starting over again with a focus on home textile design that included bedding, drapery—really, everything textile. I still had the crazy idea of focusing on fashion-inspired products. I wanted to create a signature look. I approached my design concept as a novice. I didn't think it through or use data to assess the potential. It wasn't well received by consumers in the brick-and-mortar setting. But this time, I had a better understanding of the marketplace. I created a look that I knew was unique and appealing, and this time it took off in the online marketplace. That spark led me to take a risk with e-commerce and design, creating the Lush Decor brand.

Using an e-commerce business model changed the whole dynamic of my business. We had to develop our own designs and keep inventory in our warehouse. We had always relied on buying bulk to get a better price, but with this model, we had no idea what would sell. Shipping out piece by piece instead of a thousand pieces at a time meant an entirely different internal process.

We didn't have an inventory management system or a dedicated warehouse team when we launched our first omni-channel account with Kohls.com. But I committed to shipping on time. Our little warehouse exploded with towering piles of boxes. It was literally my version of bootstrapping which I called "stiletto strapping." I wore high heels almost every day because I saw customers so often. And I spent time in the warehouse every day sorting through mountains of boxes. We had to shake the bottom boxes to loosen the top one so it would tumble down, then catch it, slap the shipping label on it, and carry it to the truck. Like a rite of passage, everyone on my team had their turn to shake the pile. It became a running joke. It was how we got by.

At the end of the year, Kohl's called and invited us to a vendor summit. They didn't share any details about the event, and we didn't have a budget for travel, so I didn't go. A few days later, a package came in the mail.

"This came from Kohls.com for you this morning." Rachel placed a box on my desk.

For the life of me, I couldn't figure out what they would have sent me. We cut it open and dug through the packing peanuts to find what looked like a statue wrapped in bubble wrap.

"What the heck is this?" I still couldn't figure it out.

But when I unwrapped it, Rachel gasped. "Rookie of the Year!"

I never expected to win an award. I read the enclosed note to Rachel. "They recognized us for our unique designs, for shipping on time, and for our independent approach to solving problems."

After Rachel left my office, I closed the door. I sat and stared at the award, inspecting every word, every feature, letting it soak into my soul. And I let a few tears of joy slide down my cheeks. I felt the entrepreneurship thread tug at my heart. That award meant everything to me. It was huge to know that we were proving our ability to perform in the e-commerce marketplace. The award served as an affirmation that we were heading in the right direction.

Once again, an unexpected spark rekindled the fire in my soul. This spark provided the confidence we needed to focus on our own brand and marketplace. After all that our little company had been through, this recognition breathed renewed hope into the entire team. I put the award out where everyone could see it.

CHAPTER 10

"**I LIKE IT.** I want to make an offer," I said.

The realtor appeared startled by my statement. "Well! Okay. Are you sure? I mean, we haven't even toured the inside yet."

I chuckled as we walked up to the front door. "It's okay. I like to make fast decisions." If I can decide to marry someone after five days, I can decide on what house to buy in a few minutes. Of course, she didn't know that about me.

I found our cape-style home with dormer windows in a quiet New Jersey neighborhood that was developed in the 1960s. After checking it out online, I knew the school system had a high rating, and the school where my son would attend pre-kindergarten was literally down the street. As long as the structure wasn't collapsing, I planned to make an offer.

"It's small at just twelve-hundred square feet, but it has potential," the agent said.

The faint musty odor that met my nose when she opened the front door transported me. I suddenly felt myself lying on a bed mat on the floor watching Dr. Xu turn out the lamp in our tiny, damp room in that basement in Beijing.

"I've lived in smaller spaces," I said with a smile.

As a single mother, I wanted to be settled into a family-oriented neighborhood before my son started school. Buying this house meant stretching financially, having barely recovered from the lawsuit, but I wanted to take this step for both of us. It was the first house I would live in since leaving my village back in China. I was ready. Part of me wanted to prove to my parents, once again, of my capability, that my way worked. Weaving the family thread into my success story was always part of my dream. My parents had come to help me with my son. I wanted to show them that my choice to stay in the US was a good one. Buying the house would establish a sense of stability in my and my son's lives as I moved to formally end my marriage.

❊

Divorce in China requires that both spouses return to the city where they married to sign papers and finalize the divorce action. It felt a bit surreal—and awkward—to return to China just for this purpose. After signing our paperwork, we left the building and paused on the outside stairs. We embraced and wished each other the best. We had an amicable divorce because we both knew we had simply grown apart. We parted as friends knowing we would continue to talk often about our son.

Wei had relocated to Beijing but made regular calls to talk with him. He also began making yearly visits to spend time with him. Wei always stayed with us during those visits. It was important that he always be part of our family.

A few months after life settled down, I arrived home in time to have dinner with my son. He hit me with a tough question.

"Momma, why do all the other kids have a dad? Why don't I have a dad? You know, who lives with us?"

My heart sank. He saw dads in the mornings and afternoons, sometimes visiting the classroom. I smiled and kissed his forehead. "Someday, my love. Someday."

❊

Daphne, a friend from the Fashion Institute who often came to visit, sat at my kitchen table one Saturday morning. Her New York attitude oozed all over me as we sipped coffee.

"You need to get on a dating website. Let's sign you up right now," she said.

"But the ink isn't even dry on my divorce papers! Can you give me a minute?" I pleaded.

But Daphne had a keen ability to read people. She knew Wei and I had grown apart well before we separated, and she saw right through my dramatic eye roll and feigned disinterest. She knew I was lonely.

She smirked and clapped with excitement. "Grab your laptop. Let's get your profile set up."

"I'm telling you right now, I'm going to be very picky," I replied. "My son is only three years old. I'm looking for someone for the two of us, not just for me."

I dove into the registration process with Daphne hovering over my shoulder, eager to learn how it all worked. After thirty minutes, I lost my patience. It was tedious; the site wanted so much detail. I knew those details were important for screening, but I just wanted to cut to the chase, literally.

"Oh, forget this," I said. "I'll work on it later."

"Okay, okay. But I'm going to keep on you to get it done," Daphne warned me.

I never told her that I gave up two more times before I finally set up my profile.

Dating proved challenging with a young child at home. But my mother and father were staying with us to help me care for my son. In China, caring for your grandchildren is a big part of the culture. My parents believed it was their duty, and they loved every minute of it. My son's command of Chinese soared. The idea of my son being bilingual thrilled me.

Despite the fact that my parents loved my son, they missed their friends and social circle back in Beijing.

"I feel trapped. It's like jail," my father complained to me one evening.

His comment sent me back to my first days in San Francisco, alone in that apartment all day. He did not feel safe venturing out beyond their daily walks through our neighborhood or to the school with my son. My parents stayed year-round now that I was single. Looking after my son kept them busy, and they had no opportunity to make friends. I could do little to help them.

"I understand," I said. But my twelve-plus hour workdays left me little time for my son, my parents, or dating. Guilt haunted me. I knew my parents would be okay, but I worried what effect my absence would have on my son.

Several months went by with quite a few random dates through the dating site. None of them piqued my interest enough for a second date. And then, late one evening, after my family had gone to bed, I felt restless and unable to sleep. I sat up in bed and scrolled around the site for something to do. That's when I got an icebreaker from Steve, a widowed attorney with no children.

I accepted his invite, and he thoughtfully chose a sushi place in my neighborhood. A few days later, we greeted each other with a hug just outside the restaurant.

"Great to meet you, Jenny. What does your family call you?"

His question made me smile and gave me a sense of relief that I didn't have to pretend to be someone I wasn't. "My name is Jing." Once we were seated at our table, our conversation started off slowly.

"My wife died four years ago." Steve fidgeted with his chopsticks while we talked. "She was an alcoholic. It was a shame. She was so young."

"I'm so sorry you went through that." I waited for him to make eye contact. "It must have been a sad and difficult time for you and your family."

Steve smiled a warm, gentle smile and nodded. I changed the subject. "So, you don't have children?"

"No, we really weren't ready. And with her addiction, it wouldn't have been good. To be honest, I've never really had much experience or interest in kids." His eyes locked on mine, watching for a response.

Ugh. Awkward. "I can understand that, given your situation." My heart sank. Steve was so easy to talk with and the most charming man I'd met in a long time. I liked him immediately. And he loved Chinese food and culture! But his feelings about children concerned me. How would he react to my son? Why couldn't he not like dogs or pizza or anything else instead?

By the end of the evening, all the awkward, first-date stuff was out of the way. Conversation came so easily. We discovered we both loved to cook, entertain, and laugh. And when we cared about someone, we cared deeply. That date marked the start of a passionate six-month dating relationship.

As the only man I was interested in, I decided to introduce Steve to Mother and my son. By then, I was falling in love with him, so my nerves were on edge. I held my breath for what felt like hours, waiting for him to pull up to my house for that first visit. When Steve met my son, his relaxed personality put my son at ease. They interacted as though they had known each other for years. Steve genuinely seemed to enjoy playing with my son. They clicked, and it seemed so natural. I exhaled.

Hallelujah!

Their connection shifted Steve's perspective of kids, and his interest blossomed along with their relationship.

Steve lived in a spacious two-bedroom condo on the Jersey Shore. Just a few months after we met, we decided he would move into my home, which mortified Mother. Our traditional Chinese culture expected that couples didn't sleep together before they were married.

One day while I was out, one of my friends from China stopped by to visit. Mother took advantage of the moment, asking my friend to translate a question to Steve.

"When are you going to get married?" A blush of color filled Steve's face when my friend delivered the question, and he laughed. We hadn't discussed it, so he wasn't sure how to respond. But Mother had gotten her message across.

The embarrassment didn't stop there for me. You know how a child can be so blunt and honest? My son really wanted a dad.

"Mom, is Uncle Steve going to be my dad?" he blurted in front of Steve.

Embarrassment flooded every inch of my body, but the warm smile on Steve's face filled my heart. The thread of love I so desperately wanted to revive had returned.

We'd known each other for six months when we got married. My decision to marry Wei took less than a week, so I figured six months of dating was an enormous improvement. Steve and I had opposite personalities; I believed his laid-back demeanor balanced my high energy and impatience.

Our wedding was a simple affair with just our closest friends and family gathered to celebrate. It was not only a big day for us as a couple but also a huge one for my three-year-old son. With infectious excitement, he told his friend, "I'm getting married too, with Mommy and Uncle Steve! We're all getting married together!" His understanding of the day, one of a child's pure innocence, brought smiles and tender laughter to all of us.

We really loved each other, and Steve loved my son as if he were his own. I sold my sweet little house soon after the wedding, and we all moved to his condo at the beach. We knew it wasn't a long-term living solution, so once the business became more stable, we bought a beautiful double lot a few blocks from the beach and started building a new home that would accommodate family and guests. My parents returned to China soon after. Life felt complete in a way I had never experienced before. It was miles away from the horror I had gone through—or so I thought.

✳

During my decade as an immigrant, the most profound shift in my life occurred the day I married Steve. His love, and the embrace of his big family, gifted me something I had yearned for all these years—a genuine sense of belonging in America. I had spent years trying to build a stable life here by contributing to the community and facing the numerous challenges that come with being an immigrant. Yet through all this, I couldn't shake off a feeling of impermanence, of feeling like an outsider in a country I desperately wanted to call home.

But then came Steve and his family. Their acceptance, their love, went beyond any cultural or national boundaries. They enveloped my son and me in a warmth and sense of belonging that was completely new to me. They opened their hearts, weaving us into the very fabric of their family. More than love, it provided a salve to the alienation and the struggle for belonging that had been constant companions in my life. The love and acceptance I received from Steve and his family shed new light on my life, filling it with peace and a deep, profound sense of belonging. I no longer stood outside looking in; I had finally found my home.

Steve's support in the naturalization process proved invaluable. Realizing that I could finally call America my home was more than just a legal formality; it created a profound shift within my heart. I finally understood that home isn't just a place; it's where you're loved and where you love in return. In this new family, I discovered parts of myself that I hadn't known before. Sharing my culture with them and embracing theirs in return, we created a beautiful blend of our worlds. It became a nurturing space where my son and I could thrive, fully embraced and supported as part of a loving family.

On the day of my naturalization ceremony, dressed in a vibrant red jacket—a nod to my Chinese heritage—I stood in a New Jersey federal building feeling a whirlwind of emotions. Red symbolized not just luck, but the rich tapestry of my Chinese and immigrant past being woven seamlessly into my American present. The seriousness of the ceremony moved me deeply coaxing a tear from my eye. This moment marked a significant step I'd never imagined on the night I first landed in San Francisco.

Faces from all walks of life filled the room, each about to embark on their own American dream. They mirrored my story of resilience and hope. My path, starting with a companion visa, then transitioning through an H1 visa journey, reflected the long and winding road faced by many legal immigrants. Becoming an American citizen was exhilarating yet tinged with the bittersweet reality of relinquishing my Chinese citizenship. In that moment, I began weaving together the best parts of my dual heritage, bridging two worlds with pride and anticipation.

The journey to this day held its share of challenges for each new citizen. The lengthy wait for legal residency, often spanning a decade or more, cast a shadow of uncertainty over many lives, leaving us unsure of our future in this country. It's a part of the immigrant story that's often unseen, yet profoundly felt.

My new identity as an Asian American meant being conscious of the balancing act between respecting my roots and adapting to my new home. America's rich diversity, its melting pot of cultures, became a part of my own story. The solemnity of the ceremony was a vivid reminder of my long journey. The scent of pine trees seemed to linger in the air, a sensory memory from my first day in America, symbolizing the start of this incredible chapter. This moment marked a turning point in my life.

❋

Once my business partner, Dan, and I finalized our buyout settlement plan, I had a clear vision to expand our ecommerce business with our new sourcing flexibility. I could see the light at the end of tunnel with steady margin growth.

My company grew so fast that I didn't have the time to step back and work on the business or to develop a strategy for sustainability. I had a very hands-on approach in the early years, overseeing everything and everyone, and I was burning out.

Steve hated his job as a litigation attorney. Every time he had to go to court, it drained him. I desperately needed help in a few areas of the operation of the company, so we decided that he should come to work for me. Our growth was crazy from launches with Amazon, Wayfair, and Target. We had to move from our original 4,000-square-foot warehouse to a 58,000-square-foot warehouse with full racking. Steve spearheaded the installation of an inventory management system.

The business had become a multi-headed monster. We needed to integrate with each customer's unique platform, our designs had to be on trend, and we had to build infrastructure to drop ship each order. Customers had become accustomed to a quick turnaround, expecting next-day delivery. No matter which direction you looked, the expectations were immense.

Within a year, I realized bringing Steve into the company was one of the worst business decisions I'd ever made. I loved Steve's laid-back personality in our personal life, but it did not fit well with my growing business. His attorney mentality, seeing everything as a warning sign instead of an opportunity, differed greatly from mine. Steve was easy-going, exactly opposite to my personality. Nothing ever happened fast enough for me, and that put us at odds. It felt like we worked twenty-four hours a day. Although we constantly talked about the business, our discussions were not productive or helpful.

Even though I owned the company, our work relationship gradually became a power struggle. At the same time, I also struggled with how to be a wife and a boss. I constantly teetered between love for Steve and frustration with our disparate approaches to business. We were tossed about in a sea of emotions where waves of his caution crashed endlessly against my ambitious drive. Every warning sign he pointed to felt like an anchor, hindering my momentum. Every opportunity I saw seemed to him like a potential pitfall. Our discussions often spiraled into storms of disagreement and misunderstanding. His caution was rooted in a place of genuine concern and an unwavering desire to protect both our business and our personal lives. But for someone like me, who perceives obstacles as mere stepping stones to greater success, it was mentally exhausting to resist his apprehension. I just wanted to explore uncharted territory for the prospect of new opportunities.

As we grappled with the bigger decisions surrounding the business, the tension between us escalated. It became evident that a business couldn't operate effectively with two decision-makers who struggled to communicate. Our team members found themselves caught in the crossfire, uncertain about whose guidance to follow. I recognized this as a significant challenge. Clearly, our communication skills were lacking and over time the resentment between us had grown, exacerbating the situation.

"We have to agree on the decisions we make. We can't move forward if we are at odds. That is why I need to have the final say." I held my breath, waiting for an explosion.

"Why do you always have to be so damned bossy?" He stormed out of my office.

We went through a really difficult period, and our situation fueled resentment for both of us. I began to realize we didn't know each other well enough to pursue this business together.

Three years into our marriage, we were arguing a lot, and it took a toll on us. We had also built a new house and moved again, adding even more stress to our lives. I felt that something wasn't right. I suggested we go to marriage therapy, but Steve didn't like the idea.

✽

One rare midsummer Sunday morning, I was delighted to linger over my coffee and not be rushing off to the office.

"Hey, I'm taking everybody to the beach for a few hours. Want to join us?" Steve asked. His parents were visiting for the weekend, and my son was eager to show off his boogie-boarding skills. It was shaping up to be a perfect beach day, but I craved some alone time.

"No, thanks. I'm going to stay here to catch up on a few emails."

I made my way to the kitchen not long after they headed out. Our living room faced east, and I loved sitting in the morning sun that streamed in through large windows on either side of the fireplace.

A vibrating buzz caught my attention as I settled in.

Ah, he left his cell phone.

I didn't typically look at Steve's phone, but when it continued to explode with text messages, instinct prodded me to peek. So, I did.

Oh my god! What the hell?

The words on the screen burned my eyes as I scrolled through a very intimate message thread between Steve and a woman who worked in our office.

"No! NO!! Damn it!!"

As I continued to scroll through the illicit exchange, a deafening silence enveloped me. My heart didn't just break; it splintered into a million shards.

The words began sinking in as tears spilled uncontrollably, not just for the betrayal but for every promise made and the unbreakable tether that I thought bound us together. I felt incredibly foolish, like I was the only one who didn't know, the last to be let in on this secret.

As I continued to read, the words blurred and they stopped making sense. I shivered, feeling oddly detached, as if I were floating outside of myself, witnessing a stranger's torment.

Frantic and reeling from yet another betrayal, I raced up the stairs and hid in the walk-in closet in our bedroom. My head spun—the room spun—as I tried to take in the shock of what I'd read. My chest tightened as I sobbed, struggling to get a breath. I thought I was having seizures.

How could he do this? How could this be happening to me?

"Jing? Where are you?" It seemed like time had been standing still when I heard Steve walk into our bedroom. He opened the closet door and saw me crouched in a corner. He tried to help me up from the floor. "Are you okay? What happened?"

"WHY?" I screamed and shoved him back. I trembled with electric anger. I could see he had no idea what I was talking about. "You! And another woman! WHY!" It wasn't a question. I just needed to scream at him to release some of the venom flowing through my veins.

"You looked at my phone?"

"It was exploding with texts," I hissed. It was impossible for me to be civil. "I thought it might be a problem with the business. But no, it was her."

"Really, Jing. It's no big deal. We're just friends, joking around, you know . . .?"

"Those texts are NOT joking." I snapped. "Get out."

"But what am I going to tell my parents right now?"

"Oh, I'm sure you can make up some kind of clever lie."

I couldn't just stuff away the massive, raw hurt and go downstairs pretending everything was fine. I couldn't hold my shit together. I just wanted to hide from everyone, especially my son.

I retreated to one of the guest bedrooms. I paced the floor as the night dragged on without mercy. I stared out the window at the black sky, the word *why* running on an endless loop in my brain.

When morning finally came, I returned to our bedroom when I heard the family downstairs preparing breakfast. My body felt heavy, burdened by the knowledge that lay heavily on my heart. I picked up the airline ticket for a flight taking off in just a few hours. Could I really step on that plane, leaving behind the smoking rubble of my marriage, to discuss business as though my world wasn't collapsing?

With a sigh that felt like it pulled from the depths of my soul, I squared my shoulders. I packed away my broken heart beneath layers of professional attire and pulled my suitcase behind me. I paused in the kitchen to kiss my son on the forehead and say my goodbyes to the family. Thankfully, my car seemed to drive itself while I cried. Lack of sleep and emotional torment left me in a zombie-like state. I don't remember how many stops I made to get coffee, but I'm sure it was too many. You know that feeling when you eat nothing and just chug lots of coffee? The jitters were unrelenting.

The meeting unfolded in a blur as my automated self performed like a well-practiced robot that could speak of margins, forecasts, and strategic alliances with a smile plastered on its face. No one seemed to notice the way my hands quivered or how my voice fell flat when discussing future plans. Underneath the polished exterior, my internal voice was stuck on a continual loop of self-blame.

Did my obsession with success drive him away? Did my assertiveness trample his spirit?

Back at the hotel after a long day, I hurried to my room. This time, however, I hurried because I was desperate to disappear. I locked myself in the room, leaving the do not disturb sign dangling on the handle.

Why couldn't you just be softer, Jenny?

The harsh self-criticism echoed in my mind.

Why couldn't you have seen him struggling under the weight of your ambition?

My thoughts spiraled, relentless in their cruelty. I crawled into the cold, impersonal hotel bed far from home, pummeled by thoughts of self-doubt and sorrow.

What could I have done differently? How has it come to this? Maybe I wasn't present enough for him?

A profound sense of failure washed over me. It became obvious I hadn't been good enough, caring enough. It seemed my own shortcomings led to this moment of despair. It was clear the thread of trust that had been so strong was not just strained; it was completely severed.

❉

By the time I returned home three days later, the shock of the situation began subsiding, allowing my emotions to settle a little bit and my mind to unlock. I didn't know where to begin or how to deal with it. My first instinct was to fix my marriage somehow, to work it out. My first marriage had gently unraveled like a delicately woven sweater, threads loosening over time until there was nothing left to salvage. But this violent, unexpected implosion left me unprepared to navigate through its wreckage. My son, the beacon of innocence amidst this chaos, unknowingly became my anchor, grounding me when despair threatened to carry me away.

This time I worried about how a divorce would affect my son and my own sense of relationship failure. Desperate for a solution, I met with the woman Steve had been seeing, attempting to seek answers, clarity, or maybe just an opportunity to gaze into the eyes of the woman who shared in my husband's deceit. Her denials, her eventual shift to blame, became a bizarre dance of the surreal with the painfully real. Business and emotions became a complex tangle, forcing me to find my way through potential legal repercussions while nursing a bleeding heart.

The ensuing days were a blur of legal consultations, hushed conversations, and sleepless nights, with my emotions swinging like a pendulum between anger, sadness, and desolation. I had taken screenshots of all the texts and sent them to myself. I knew I would never see them again otherwise. Eventually, resolutions were drawn, settlements made, and we orchestrated the other woman's departure as smoothly as possible given the circumstances. That chapter with her closed, yet the pain of broken trust lingered.

Tears blurred my vision as I tried to explain to my son the seismic shift thrust upon our family. Divorce felt like a failure, a stark contrast to the cohesive family image I'd always aspired to provide.

His gentle yet unexpectedly mature response took me aback. "You're not a failure, Mom." And within those simple words, comfort unfurled, reassuring yet bitterly sweet.

Our journey wasn't neat or linear. It took us years to work through the divorce process and settle on an amicable solution. We fumbled, we stumbled, we navigated through a labyrinth of emotions and adjustments. My son's teenage years, vibrant with rebellions and discoveries, were often a mirror to my own internal turmoil.

"Mom, what you're doing is really impressive." His words concealed my vulnerability, showing me that my shortcomings were not as transparent as I feared.

In the rubble of the marriage, Steve and I forged an unexpected friendship, salvaging a sanctuary for our son. Two houses, side by side, became our son's stable ground, his domains to navigate freely. It was a solution born out of desperation, yet it blossomed into a framework that minimized the chaos inflicted on his world by our separation.

Arguments, disagreements, and silent treatments found their place between our moments of laughter and shared memories for my son and me. We didn't have all the answers, and some days it felt like we had none at all. But our mother-son relationship became a testament to evolving, to building bridges over gaps of misunderstandings and hurt feelings.

In the confines of my therapist's office, I allowed myself to be vulnerable, exploring the depth of my pain and acknowledging the gnawing fear of whether I could ever rebuild from these ruins, and mend that severed thread of trust. I questioned everything—my worth, my role, the viability of my marriage, and how to safeguard my son's emotional well-being.

As I started to pick up the fragments of my broken self, a profound realization dawned upon me: forgiveness was not a gift to my ex-husband or this woman, but a balm for my own wounded soul. It offered a release; a letting go to allow light into my future. It required a daily commitment, a conscious choice to unshackle myself from bitterness. I began to reconstruct my life, not as it was, but shaping it into a new form that reflected my journey, my growth, and my pain.

I grappled with the decision to share this deeply personal story, one that is intricately tied to my heart and our family. I've asked myself time and time again, "Why do you want to share it?"

Through countless hours of individual therapy and couples' counseling during my healing journey, the answer became clear. I realized there are many people out there, just like me and just like us, facing the same struggles and heartaches. I also know the profound pain and suffering that can persist if we remain trapped in our wounded selves. However, I've also experienced the relief, the growth, and the newfound lightness that forgiveness—especially self-forgiveness—can bring. Self-compassion and self-worth are new threads I unearthed in the process. I am learning how important they are and that I must weave them into my life and my dreams for my future.

I share this story for those who are still trying to find their way out, those who may be questioning if there's a way forward. I want you to know you are not alone, and that you too can find your way to a place of healing, growth, and ultimately a better version of yourself.

CHAPTER 11

HAVE YOU EVER reached the point of complete burnout? Burnout snuck up on me, accumulating like snowflakes in a blizzard, despite the work I was doing to redefine myself. Burnout left me emotionally numb and drained down to my last few drops of energy. I had hoped I would never see rock bottom again. It was a little different this time, but I recognized it just the same. I still worked all the time and neglected to pay enough attention to myself.

One night, after my son fell asleep, I took the stairs up to my bedroom. But something felt wrong. Very wrong. I couldn't breathe and my strength bled away.

This is really bad.

Fighting to reach the top step, I fell forward into the hallway to avoid tumbling backward.

Am I having a heart attack?

With cellphone in hand, I lay on the floor, suffocating in deep fear.

Am I dying? Should I call 911?

In my early forties, I had never been so scared in my life. Lying flat on my back gave me some physical relief, but my heart and mind raced on. I closed my eyes and tried to calm myself. At some point, I either passed out or drifted off to sleep.

First thing in the morning, I called my doctor's office. After explaining my episode to the nurse, she suggested I come right in. My pulse and blood pressure were elevated but not into the danger zone. Sitting alone in the exam room, I felt every inch of my mortality.

"Good morning, Jenny. I understand you had a scare last night. Tell me what happened," the doctor said.

I liked my doctor. He always cut right to the chase. My kind of guy. As I explained my episode, he asked what had been happening in my personal and professional life.

"It sounds like you may have had a panic attack," he said, after I filled him in. "Given what you've been through, this is most likely a mental stress issue."

"Huh. Well, I need to be mentally stable for my son. And my business. What are my options?"

The doctor handed me a prescription. "This medicine will help you cope and manage your stress."

I hate pills and medication. They're always a last resort because I feel as though they suppress the real me. I believed I was strong and didn't need them. I'm not a fan of Chinese medicine either, and for most of my life, I never needed it. I wanted to control my own mind and didn't want to be numbed out. To me, taking medicine was almost like accepting defeat. But I had to accept that life was too much for me at that moment. I had to face reality and focus on getting better.

When I told the doctor my concerns, he said, "Don't worry. It's not a long-term solution. You need to focus on getting your physical and emotional health back on track."

The scare I experienced was enough. I never wanted to feel like that again. My son and my business were too important to take such a risk. I filled the prescription on my way to my office.

This degree of burnout drew me into unfamiliar territory. I had to find help. I always found exercise to be a great stress reliever, but I lacked the self-discipline to go to a gym regularly. Later that morning, after a brief online search, I found a personal trainer and called him. His gym was just a few blocks away, so I went in for an assessment. I liked his approach and felt confident he could hold me accountable.

"Okay. Let's get started tomorrow," I said.

He looked surprised by my desire to jump right in, but this new chapter in my life couldn't wait. I'd never had to work at being healthy or fit before.

For the next three months, I worked with the trainer and took medication. Then I took myself off the pills. My health and stress levels had improved, giving me more energy and a better attitude. Exercise became a crucial tool for managing my stress, but I still struggled to get on the other side of the emotional burden I carried.

My next call was to my therapist.

Success has a way of making you think you are invincible. No matter how successful you are in life and business, when you need help, you need help. For me, help came from my doctor, a personal trainer, a therapist, and my willingness to accept that I needed all of it.

✳

I hate spam emails. We all do, I guess. They send me ripping through my inbox, rapidly deleting anything that even remotely resembles junk. In late 2016, I noticed an uptick in emails and phone calls asking if I wanted to sell my business. Most of them were from private equity firms. I didn't even know what private equity was, so I ignored them. I was too busy trying to maintain control of my three-headed monster of a company to bother with something I didn't understand.

But my frustration reached a new high one afternoon as I explored expansion options. We were struggling to keep pace with customer demand in our current space, and a bigger warehouse would require a significant investment. I felt backed into a corner.

Head in my hands, I stared mindlessly at a patch of wood grain peeking through the piles of paperwork on my desk. The sound of a new email attracted my gaze. Ugh, another one. This time though, just for the hell of it, I did a quick online search. They were a big private equity firm in Boston.

Huh. They're legit.

Figuring I had nothing to lose, I replied and scheduled a call during my drive home after work. The man who called asked questions about my business performance numbers.

"Um, are you sure that's correct?" he asked after I gave him what he requested.

"Yes, I am sure. We've never had commercial debt. Our margins are solid."

His questions turned me off. I knew almost nothing about private equity, but I knew my business numbers inside and out. Business bankers had always pushed me to get loans, but I hated the idea. I think it was my Asian mindset. We don't like to borrow money. Some would consider that mindset an obstacle, and it may have held me back. But I funded our growth on my own, my version of stiletto strapping, and that made me proud. After buying out my first two partners, my trust level was in the toilet, so I became even more adamant about self-funding our growth. That meant having the margin to support it.

I like to joke that I design a beautiful product and a beautiful margin too.

"Well, that's pretty amazing. We don't see numbers like that; it's very rare. Especially on the profit side. Your profit margin is rather unheard of in your industry." This guy was just an associate analyst tasked with gathering information and he struggled to hide his excitement. He asked me to send him some accounting reports and recommended I meet with the managing director right away.

Within a week, the managing director called to schedule a meeting with me to review his calculations.

"Take a look," he said, pushing a paper in front of me. "This represents the value of your company."

I scanned the evaluation. "Wow!" Now it was my turn to hide my excitement. I didn't realize what went into a business valuation. The number he showed me made it hard to refuse their offer to sell my company. "So how would this work if I were to go ahead?"

"I recommend getting an investment banker to help you. Ted is a banker I've worked with. Here's his business card."

During our call a few days later, Ted also got very excited. He said we could sell my company within three months. And that's where it all stopped. That sensation of not being able to breathe crept in. I thanked Ted for his time and hung up.

The thought of selling my company in less than three months scared the crap out of me. I didn't understand enough to make that kind of decision. Plus, I was still recovering from burnout, I had no support, and I was learning everything on the job. I simply couldn't see very far ahead. At this point you know how much I like to make fast decisions, but at that time, instinct told me not to rush. Risk-taking was something I loved, but my intuition thread had strengthened considerably over the years. I felt I needed to be more responsible, not just for me but for my team. I needed to treat this business like my child.

The fact that everyone I spoke to seemed "so excited" meant only one thing: with no mentors, no advisers, no peers to guide me, I had to learn everything I could about private equity before I took another step. I interviewed bankers on my own, trying to make sense of how to select one I could trust. I'd never had a mentor before, but my intuition guided me to be patient and wait for the person who wanted to help me, not just make money.

That's when I met Charlie. Something about him put me at ease. Our conversation felt like a sincere exchange. He was patient and knowledgeable, and I sensed his integrity.

"I'm in no hurry to do this," I said. "I have too much to learn about private equity investors." I watched his face, waiting for the smirk of disappointment all the others had given me.

Charlie smiled and nodded in agreement. "That makes sense, Jenny."

I exhaled. We agreed to work together, and we've worked together ever since.

Charlie never pushed me to sell my business. He explained the pros and cons so I could decide for myself. For the next year, without a single complaint, Charlie made the hour-and-a-half round trip drive every week to meet with me. We would meet at a small coffee shop in my city. I still smile every time I stop by that coffee shop and see the table where we spent hours together. I felt comfortable asking all kinds of financial questions. He answered with care and never let me feel ignorant. He held my hand for a full year, teaching me every aspect of private equity—basically providing me with the equivalent of a mini-MBA. His support allowed me to feel less stupid and vulnerable. By the end of that year, we had a business relationship built on rock-solid trust. Charlie became the mentor and trusted friend I had always needed. The business aspect of my thread of trust was restored, and it felt really good.

Doing a lot of homework has always helped me. Knowledge really is power. My research helped me realize I just needed to do my part to make an equity partnership work. That meant being a responsible partner, keeping the other party in the loop, and being a collaborative participant. That meant assuming responsibility for the team and accepting guidance from my partners so we could take risks together. My job was to steer the ship in the right direction. From my perspective, the most important objective was maintaining integrity in the partnership based on strong character and competency.

"Are you ready to jump in?" Charlie smiled, already knowing the answer.

"Yes. I'm ready. I know what I want and what I can offer."

"Good. Now let's go find the perfect partner."

Interviewing private equity investors was almost like speed dating. It involved non-stop talking to investor after investor. Our list included over fifty firms. Through each round we trimmed down, first to twenty, then ten, then six. The final round left us with three top offers. I thought they all seemed pretty good.

But anxiety crept in, leaving me to wonder how I would make the final decision. To help calm my fears, I asked Charlie for the worst-case scenario, the worst outcome should a partnership fail. Once Charlie explained the possible pitfalls, I was ready to move forward.

We were down to the last round of in-person meetings with three private equity firms. It was time to make my decision. It wasn't hard.

Sam, the owner of one of the final three firms, greeted me with a young woman by his side. "Good morning, Jenny. I'd like you to meet my daughter. She just graduated from high school and is heading to college in the fall. I wanted her to meet you and to learn firsthand about how private equity works."

In the world of private equity, women are rare on both sides of the table. At the time I wrote this book, women were receiving only 2.1 percent of venture capital funding, with immigrants and women of color receiving less than 1 percent of that amount. In my mind, Sam showed his support of women by exposing his daughter to our discussions. I had been the only woman in the room through this entire process until that day. It was the tipping point for my decision to work with Sam.

After I made my decision, Charlie studied my face. "You don't look happy, Jenny. Are you okay with your decision?"

"Well, half of me is relieved, you know? But half of me is nervous too." I had heard plenty of private equity horror stories about lousy deals and corrupt firms. "I'm not 100 percent sure . . ." My mind raced through the details again.

"I'll be honest with you, Jenny. It's like a marriage," Charlie said. "You will never be 100 percent sure."

We both laughed. I reminded myself that the deal gave me more financial stability than I'd ever had, and a partner to work with—a real partner this time.

"I am confident that my company has a lot of potential, so if we focus on growth, we'll do well," I said, even though I still felt a little nervous about taking the money. I understood that in private equity deals, it's not just what you receive in the exchange but what you deliver to ensure the investors see a return. My newest thread was collaboration. It changed the way I approached business from that point forward.

My redefined role included building a mutually beneficial relationship, just like I had learned to build mutually beneficial business exchanges throughout my career. Finalizing the transaction with Sam as my private equity partner marked a huge milestone for me. The financial relief and stability meant I didn't have to worry about my business the same way. All my life, I'd been in survival mode. I never had time to think about anything more than growing the business.

Before partnering with the private equity firm, I was burned out. My business was experiencing rapid growth, and I didn't have the leadership skills or understanding to manage it well. My work schedule was crazy, and my personal life was in shambles. Looking back, I realize I hadn't fully matured as a person. With my head so deep in the business, I never really stepped back to look at my leadership skills. I lacked the time and the resources.

All that changed with the stroke of a pen.

Sitting alone in my office after signing our agreement, I reflected on how I grew up and all the threads I had untangled. Mother thought I would never support myself or succeed by doing things my own way. Opting for night college, moving to Beijing, and starting businesses were risky, yet I proved I could do it, even when I had nothing but roadblocks in my way. I always wanted to exceed my mother's expectations because I knew it would make her happy. I believed I could do it, and I could do it a lot better than anyone might think.

Finalizing the transaction with my private equity partner marked a pivotal moment in my life's journey. It not only brought financial relief but also ushered in newfound stability, lifting the weight of worries from my relentless pursuit of business success. Throughout the years I had spent in survival mode, I directed my focus toward propelling the business forward. However, this partnership triggered a profound transformation within me, compelling me to shift from a business-centric mindset to a people-centric one.

Previously, my unwavering dedication to the business actually hindered my ability to embrace genuine leadership. This transformation was about the evolution of my business as well as my personal growth, signifying my transition from being a boss to becoming a true leader.

In hindsight, I wish I had possessed these profound leadership insights much earlier in my life.

I shared the impactful story of my former employer and mentor, Dr. Xu, because her influence played a pivotal role in shaping the trajectory of my life. In return for her guidance, I devoted myself to her spa business, an experience that imparted a profound lesson about the significance of elevating, mentoring, and inspiring others.

For me, creating a positive work culture came to mean nurturing an environment characterized by openness, transparency, empathy, and trust. Granting individuals the autonomy to transcend their perceived limitations allowed them to surpass not only their own expectations but also mine. Letting go of control led to remarkable growth and transformation.

❋

I am enough. Through all I have experienced and all I have learned; the most important lesson is that I am enough. My journey from the small village of my birth to this moment feels almost surreal, yet knowing what I have done allows me to see what I am capable of doing. I have a sense of purpose for what comes next.

I hope sharing my story inspires women, immigrants, and aspiring entrepreneurs with a vision. I hope it opens opportunities for them.

I have the privilege of representing all of you because I *am* all of you. I know full well the harsh landscape of business and that being a woman and an immigrant can be incredibly challenging no matter what you bring to the table. I firmly believe that no matter where you are from, no matter what dream pulses in your heart, with grit and resilience, you can ascend.Remember, threads of experience, learning, and growth are everywhere if you look for them. Pick up a thread, any thread, and weave it into your life. See how it strengthens the fabric of your life and pulls your dreams together. I began my journey as a dream weaver at the age six, all because I wanted ice cube treats. Since that time, I continued to stumble upon the threads necessary to weave my dreams. I am amazed at the power they have to cushion me in tough times and support me at all times. Some surprised me, like my Jinglish thread. Who knew I'd need that one? The thread of collaboration took a bit longer to find, but it allowed me to weave the dream of a successful business.

Weaving dreams is a skill I hope you learn and continue to hone. Your unique tapestry can be beautiful too, no matter your gender, age, country of origin, or the enormity of your vision.

FINAL THOUGHTS

COMING FULL CIRCLE in what seems like a short time is both unbelievable and fulfilling. I now sit on the board of the Home Fashion Products Association and take my turn evaluating student portfolios in the conference room at the Fashion Institute. It is incredibly satisfying to donate funds to support the same scholarship I received all those years ago.

When a young woman who is hoping to secure a scholarship brings her portfolio into the room, I see myself walking in for the first time. I can see how nervous she is, and it brings me back to my experience. I try to give her confidence during her presentation by saying things like, "By the way, you are very talented," "You own this," and "All you need is the confidence."

As a former recipient and now as a panelist granting this award, I've sat on both sides of the table. I'm passionate about helping young people who have a desire to succeed. I've received so much encouragement over the course of my career. Encouraging others satisfies my soul.

As I bring this chapter of my life to a close, it's not merely the end of a segment in a book; it's a deep and therapeutic release for my soul. This journey has been a profound exploration of every facet of my being. I've embraced it all—the joys, the pains, the triumphs, and the moments of despair. This path has taught me to embrace every aspect of myself. It wrapped me in a tapestry of experience both beautiful and the flawed, taught me how to live in harmony with every thread. There's been pain, yes, but also immense gratitude. When I look back now, I realize I was always exactly where I needed to be.

Without Wei, I might never have found my way to the US. Without the betrayal of my business partner, I might never have realized the full extent of my strength and ability to grow Lush Decor Home into a thriving business. Without Steve and his family, I might not have felt as at home in America as I do now, and my son might not have had the wonderful second father he deserves.

I'm sharing my story not as a tale of flawless success but to offer an authentic, unvarnished glimpse into my life. It's been a journey of soaring highs and heartbreaking lows, moments of crystal-clear clarity, and periods of doubt. Through it all, I've realized that each experience, regardless of how painful or challenging, has played a part in shaping who I am.

As you come to the end of my story, I hope you see it not just as a recounting of my life but as a companion to yours. May it inspire you to face your own challenges, not as insurmountable obstacles but as opportunities for growth and self-discovery.

I share these experiences with you in all their raw honesty, hoping to provide comfort in your moments of uncertainty. Remember, life isn't about avoiding challenges; it's about confronting them and emerging stronger.

As we part with these words, I hope the resilience and hope I've found in my journey inspires you. For those who wrestle with their own challenges, who think surrender is the only option, feel scared to take the next step, or find themselves tangled in life's complexities, know this: within you lies all the strength you need. Even if it isn't apparent right now, trust in your inner fortitude and your instincts. Take it one step at a time, one thread at a time, and weave your dreams. You are a dream weaver too.

ACKNOWLEDGMENTS

I N 2018, AT the ten-year mark of Lush Decor, I achieved something I had dreamed about since I was six years old—I sold a portion of the business to TZP Group and gained financial freedom. On one side, I felt like I had realized my lifelong dream, the one that started when I wanted to buy ice cream without having to ask my parents. I thought reaching this point would bring me endless happiness. But to my surprise, it didn't. Instead, I felt empty.

It was a confusing and humbling moment. I had worked so hard to get to this milestone, but instead of fulfillment, I was left asking, "Now what?" To find clarity, I decided to bring my son back to the tiny village in China where I was born—a village without electricity, where I spent my childhood. I needed to reconnect with my roots, to remember where I came from.

When I came back from that trip, I knew I needed to dig deeper into my story, to uncover the threads that had brought me from that curious little girl in a village with no amenities to where I was now. I started to reflect on the moments that shaped me, even the ones I'd tried to bury—the moments of shame, guilt, self-doubt, and heartbreak.

Growing up in that village, I was always curious about the world beyond the boundaries of what I knew. I remember being in high school and hearing the story of a woman who came from a similar background as mine. She left her village, moved to a big city, worked in a factory, and eventually built her own business. Her success planted a seed of possibility in my mind: *If she can do it, so can I.*

That belief became my foundation. It gave me the courage to leave my village, move to Beijing, and take my first steps toward building something bigger. I worked as a hotel maid, an esthetician, and even started a few small businesses. At 26, I took an even bigger leap and moved to the U.S. with barely any English. I worked as a nanny and, during that time, discovered my passion for fashion and home decor. That passion eventually led me to start Lush Decor, which grew into a $100M revenue business.

But writing this book wasn't just about the successes. It was about revisiting the parts of my journey I had hidden away—the shame I felt cleaning toilets as a hotel maid, the guilt of dragging my son through two divorces, the harsh self-judgment I placed on myself for never feeling "enough." It was about facing the resentment I held, the betrayal I carried, and the tough walls I built around myself.

Thread by thread, I pulled those pieces of my story out. I faced them, acknowledged them, and, slowly, began to accept them. Along the way, I realized this wasn't just my story—it reflected the stories of so many women. Entrepreneurs, working moms, immigrants, Asian Americans, women navigating failed relationships, and everyone who has ever doubted themselves or felt the weight of their dreams.

This book isn't just my story—it's *our* story.

To **Susan Baracco**, my collaborator and ghostwriter, you weren't just someone who helped me put words to the page—you were my therapist through this process. You encouraged me to dig deep, to be vulnerable, and to embrace the messy truth of my life. Thank you for helping me tell this story authentically.

To **Indigo River Publishing and Simon & Schuster**, thank you for believing in *Dream Weaver* and helping bring my story to life.

To **my Lush Decor team**—past and present—thank you for taking this roller-coaster journey with me. What we built together was never just about home décor; it was about creating something far deeper—inspired life, a *home for dreams*. Lush Decor isn't just a business to me; it's the vehicle that helped me find the purpose of work and the meaning of leadership. It taught me that true wealth isn't just measured in revenue or reach—it's in the people who dared to build alongside you, even when the road was uncertain.

To **my mom and dad,** thank you for loving me in the best way you knew how. I know I was often resentful and stubborn, but I see now that your love, even if it wasn't the way I wanted, came from a deep place. You carried so much of your own traditions and baggage, yet you tried your best.

To **my grandmother,** who taught me how to weave fabric, you were my first inspiration. The sound of the loom, your petite feet working the pedals despite the pain of bound feet, and the rhythm of your hands wove stories that mesmerized me. That loom unlocked my dreams, and every fabric I've touched since has reminded me of my roots. This book honors you and the lessons you passed down to me—to weave life's threads into something beautiful.

To **my son,** your words on the jacket brought me to tears (okay, maybe a lot of tears). The way you described me—stubborn, bold, brave, insane, and the best mom—is so you, balancing humor and heart in a way only you can. You've seen every side of me, and yet, you still see me as your biggest inspiration. That means more than anything else in the world. You didn't just survive the chaos of our unconventional family—you embraced it with love, strength, and that sharp wit I adore. Three Christmases—your words, not mine—might have been a win-win, but having you as my son is the ultimate win for me. Thank you for loving me through all my flaws, cheering me on, and reminding me that even through life's twists and turns, we are so blessed. You're my greatest joy, my proudest achievement, and my biggest inspiration.

To **Jai,** my chief of staff, thank you for making this entire journey so enjoyable. Your steady support, calm demeanor, and ability to manage a million things at once have been invaluable. I couldn't have done this without you.

To **my friends**, whether it was through remote happy hours during COVID or offering advice and encouragement along the way, you've always been there for me. To my YPO, WPO, EOY, and Gold House families, thank you for constantly inspiring me, lifting me up, and giving me courage when I needed it most. I love you all and am endlessly grateful for your friendship and support.

To **my two ex-husbands**, thank you for being amazing fathers to our son. Thank you for letting go of resentment, forgiving, and continuing to be part of my life and his. It is a gift to have both of you in our lives, and I am grateful for that.

To **Chuck**, thank you for opening the door to the world of private equity—a world that, at first, felt foreign to me, but ultimately became a classroom in courage, conviction, and clarity. You taught me that numbers may tell the story, but people give it meaning. To all the partners and believers who stood beside me in the hard seasons—thank you for your trust, your patience, and your belief in the power of reinvention, and for helping me to transform an exit into a rebirth, a setback into a stage, and a business into a legacy.

To everyone who supported me along the way, thank you from the bottom of my heart. This journey has been far from perfect, but it's been mine, and I'm grateful to share it with you.

This is *Dream Weaver*. This is my story. And this is *our* story.

PHOTOS

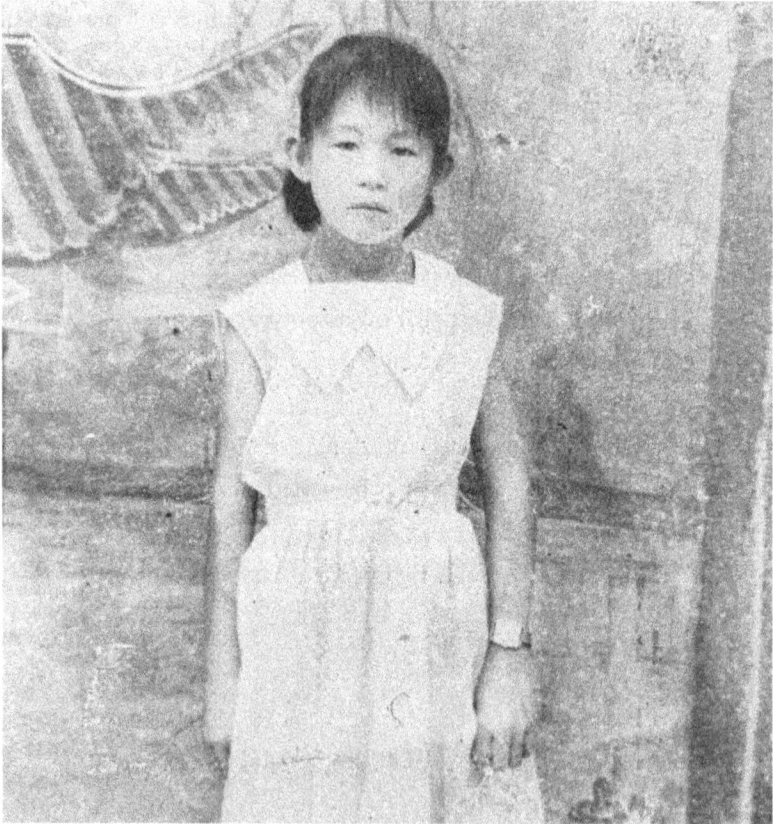

Jenny at 8, dressed in borrowed clothes and a prop watch. Taken by a photographer in a neighboring village.

Jenny's childhood village of Caolou in Shandong Province, China.

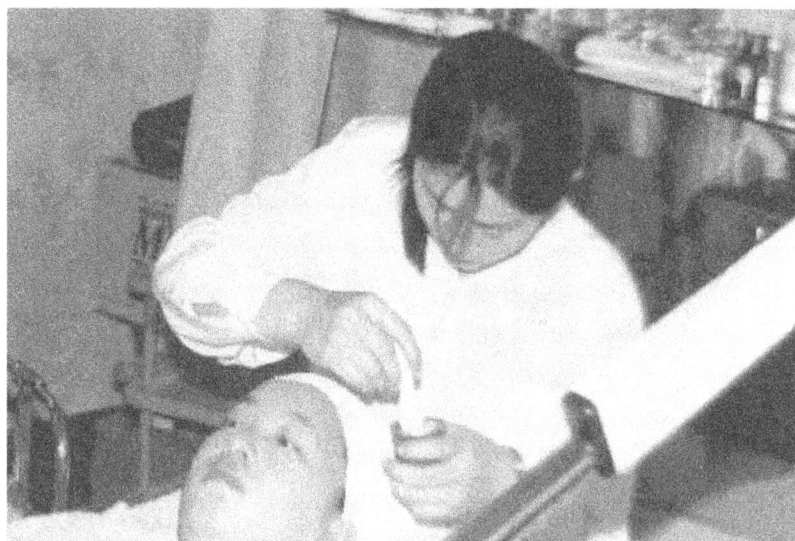

Giving facials in Beijing, in 1992.

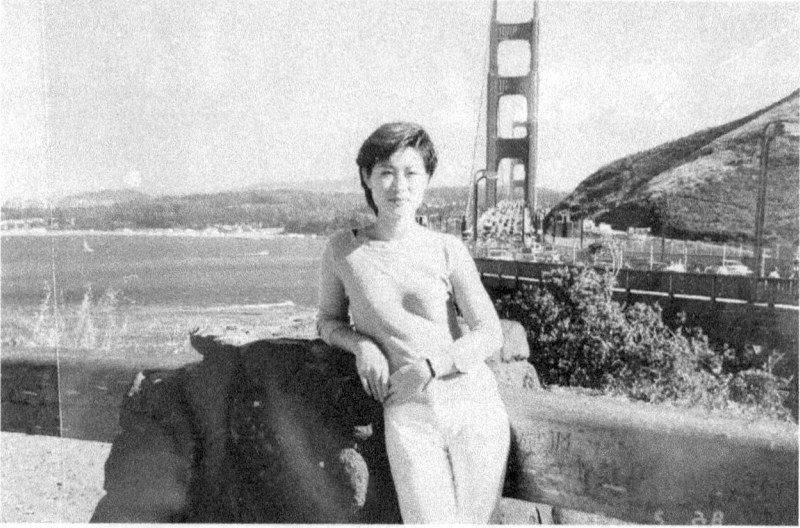

Jenny in San Francisco in 1999.

Graduation from the Fashion Institute of Technology in 2005.

Jenny and her son at Belmar Beach in New Jersey in 2014.

Jenny received the EY Entrepreneur of the Year Award in 2019.

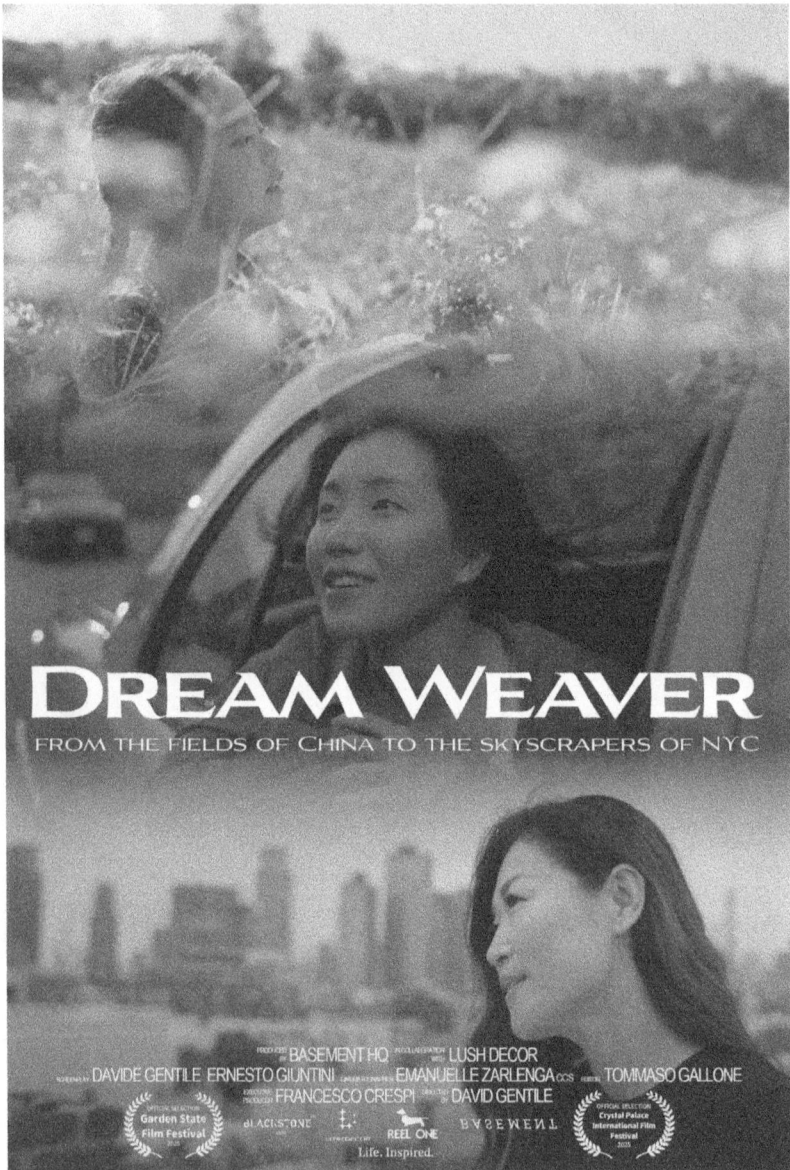

2024 Venice International Film Festival, short film poster.

✦

ABOUT THE AUTHOR

WOULD YOU BELIEVE that a girl from a remote village in Shandong, China without electricity or basic amenities, could one day build an over 100-million-dollar profitable revenue business? This is my story—my journey from humble beginnings to the forefront of entrepreneurship and empowerment.

My early years were driven by an unwavering determination to transform my family's fate. From working as a hotel maid, an esthetician, to running a dry-cleaning business, and even launching a matchmaking service for successful women, each role became a stepping stone toward a bigger dream. This adventure took a daring turn when I moved to the United States in my mid-20s, with limited English, beginning as a nanny before pursuing design studies.

The real test came in 2008, during the financial crisis. With a one-year-old by my side and on the brink of single motherhood, I founded Lush Decor Home. My path was not easy, with challenges like business betrayals, two amicable divorces, and a leap into the unknown world of private equity for my first business exit. Despite starting with no knowledge of "PE," I navigated my way to financial freedom, eventually passing the torch to a talented leadership team, now led by a woman CEO, as I embraced the role of Chairwoman of the Board.

This experience has become a story of more than overcoming challenges; it is one of resilience, growth, and rising after countless setbacks.

Today, I am a committed advocate for women and girls worldwide. Through writing *Dream Weaver: Finding Strength and Purpose in Life's Twists and Turns*, my mission is to bring hope and strength to others navigating their own paths.

Inspired by this journey, Dream Weaver, a short film based on my memoir, debuted at the 2024 Venice Film Festival with the goal of inspiring audiences around the world. To bring everything full circle, I established the Dream Weavers Foundation on a mission to empower women to dream beyond their circumstances.

As a champion for female entrepreneurs, I am a founding member of USPAACC's Women Initiative Strategic Empowerment (WISE) and the Jenny Jing Zhu Collective in partnership with Gold House. Additionally, I am a proud board member of the Women Presidents Organization (WPO), the Young Presidents Organization (YPO), and served on the board of the China Institute in America.

My determination earned me EY's New Jersey Entrepreneur of the Year Award and a national nomination in the consumer category in 2019, as well as the honor of being inducted into the Enterprising Women Hall of Fame in 2024 after receiving the Enterprising Women of the Year Award in 2021. In both 2021 and 2022, Lush Decor was recognized as one of the 50 Fastest Growing Women-Owned/Led Companies by the WPO. Inc. Magazine also honored Triangle Home Fashions | Lush Decor as a Top 500 Fastest Growing Company in 2022.

For media and speaking engagement requests, please contact Jai Guess at jai@dreamweavers.org

For more about Jenny Jing Zhu visit JennyJingZhu.com

For more on Dream Weavers Foundation visit DreamWeavers.org

For more on Lush Decor visit LushDecor.com.

www.ingramcontent.com/pod-product-compliance
Lightning Source LLC
Chambersburg PA
CBHW051727090426
42738CB00010B/2134